DIALOGUE ON A
DIFFICULT ISSUE

Congregations Talking about Homosexuality

BETH ANN GAEDE, EDITOR

An Alban Institute Publication

Scripture quotations are from the New Revised Standard Version of the Bible, copyright © 1989 by the Division of Christian Education of the National Council of the Churches of Christ in the United States of America. Used by permission. All rights reserved.

Library of Congress Catalog Number 97-78128
ISBN 1-56699-198-6

CONTENTS

Congregations are asked from time to time to decide whether to discuss controversial issues and then whether to go public with the outcome of that discussion. In the years I have been in ordained ministry, I have worked with congregations struggling with such issues as these:

- Shall we support a proposition on the state ballot to remove housing covenants from property deeds that segregate the races?
- Shall we write a letter to the president of the United States expressing dismay about the incursion of U.S. troops into Cambodia?
- Shall we help fund our pastor's trip to Selma, Alabama, to march in support of voting rights for blacks?
- Shall we take a stand on the right of individuals or couples to make a decision to abort a fetus?

In all these cases, it was difficult to decide even whether to talk about the issues. Some congregations approach potential controversy with relative ease. These faith communities are comfortable with their identity as a congregation that takes stands on private and social ethical issues. Other congregations (in fact, most congregations) affirm peoples' right to hold a diversity of opinions but believe congregations should not take stands on social issues. For whatever reasons, even when there is substantial agreement among members, discussions about issues relating to social policy make most religious folk nervous. Most members of faith communities do not like to take stands on social issues, even though the congregation's and denomination's history, tradition, understandings of biblical authority, and values demand that Christians and Jews speak out when their neighbor is suffering because of someone else's actions. This means that at least occasionally, congregations cannot avoid dealing with difficult issues.

This is a book about addressing the issue of homosexuality and about seven congregations that have struggled with the question of whether to state publicly that homosexuals are welcome to participate in the life of the congregation. The underlying question asked in this book is, Should a congregation talk publicly about value-laden issues such as homosexuality? Or, to ask an even more difficult question, Should a congregation be put in a position of making a decision about whether it will be on record as affirming homosexuals?

Reasons to Say Yes

There are good reasons for saying yes to these questions.

- Churches and synagogues have always had a point of view, something to say about right and wrong. Thou shalt not kill, do not commit adultery, do unto others as you would have them do unto you, and so forth, are basic teachings of faith communities.
- Many religious authorities, including the Bible itself, come down rather clearly on issues of morality.
- What is church about, anyway, if it is not a community of people coming together to ask, What does God require of us? and then audaciously trying to answer that question?
- One purpose of the church or synagogue is to challenge people to be responsive and accountable. It asks us to do more, to do better than we now do.

Reasons for Saying No

There are also good reasons for saying no.

- Many people in congregations become anxious about any issue on which there is no consensus. Consequently, some people do and say atrocious things when they are asked to reflect on difficult subjects.

- Usually losses (of members, tranquillity, order) accompany discussion of anxiety-producing topics. Why, then, provoke people? Why put communities in danger of such loss?
- One of the purposes of the church or synagogue is to help people find a calm center in their lives. Discussion about controversy makes it difficult and sometimes impossible to find that calm center.

Which is a congregation to focus on: calm center or challenge? If the answer is both, then how do we live with that paradox? Do we strive for calm center on Monday, Wednesday, and Friday, and challenge on Tuesday, Thursday, and Saturday? Do we try to find a balance between calm center and challenge by incorporating just enough of each into our faith community so one does not overwhelm the other? Or perhaps we just change our focus periodically to keep us involved in both calm and challenge, given that it does not seem feasible to do both at the same time.

The trick in a congregation is to answer the question, When do we challenge and when do we give comfort? I believe it is easier to answer this question with regard to individuals within the church or synagogue than it is to answer it in relation to the whole congregation. When we attempt to address the question regarding an individual, we can first think about what is going on in the person's life at that moment. If the person is experiencing tension at home or dealing with grief or other transitions, we might decide not to introduce the person to another stressful situation at this time. But when we are assessing a congregation, we have to assess not only the congregation as a whole but all the individuals within it. And some of those individuals may be stressed to the max, others may not have much stress in their lives, and yet others may have plenty of stress but still be able to take on one more thing. How can we know where the entire congregation is?

Some congregations set their stress-tolerance limit at the lowest possible level for fear of increasing the anxiety level of those who are already anxious. The problem with this strategy, of course, is that there will never be a day when everyone will be ready to deal with more stress. The best we can hope for is to pick a time when enough of us are ready and willing and able to carry those who are not ready or not quite ready at this time. (I do not know of congregations that deliberately set

their stress level at high all the time and hold it there. Such a congregation might exist, but if it does, it is outside my experience.)

   This book is less about the biblical, theological, and ethical reasons
for taking a position on the issue of homosexuality than it is a demonstration of how a congregation might go about raising and dealing with
the issue. It will help you decide specifically whether to move ahead
with a public discussion. You might find it helpful to review the final
chapter before reading the seven case studies in part 2 of the book, because it will give you a framework through which to review the cases
and offers general guidelines for deciding whether now is the time to
begin a conversation.

   The authors of these chapters and the members of the churches of
which the authors are a part have invested themselves deeply in their
quest to be faithful to their understanding of God's Word. Their invest-
ments did not necessarily allow everyone to be a "winner." Whether
participants perceived themselves as "winners" or "losers," the conversation required hard work. Some people paid dearly for their attempts to
be faithful.

   As I read these chapters, I identified both with those who struggled
to bring about what they believed to be greater justice and with those
who sought to maintain what they believed to be the core of their faith.
The struggle to be clear and fair, to hold high standards, and to reflect
on and even consider changing those standards—all at the same time—is
awesomely difficult. What I have learned is that whatever the specific
ingredients of the challenge, it is possible to change and grow. I sincere-
ly thank those who have witnessed here to the strength of faith communities and the ability of those communities to function as crucibles in
which faithful people can test and invigorate their faith.

                                                      — Speed Leas

PREFACE

The concept of sexuality is a relatively new addition to our understanding of the human. It was not until the late nineteenth century that researchers began to study sex in a scientific way. Gradually "sexuality" emerged to embrace all aspects of a person that are affected by being male or female.[1] Since the mid-1970s, due to this rise of scientific study and developments in biblical studies, sexuality and homosexuality in particular have been a more frequent topic of discussion within Christian denominations and congregations. Unfortunately, these discussions are often painful for participants, whether those involved in the conversation understand homosexuality to be clearly immoral, view homosexuality as another one of God's good gifts, or are not sure what to think. It is because many congregations have found homosexuality a difficult topic to discuss that the Alban Institute put together *Congregations Talking about Homosexuality*. We want to help congregations become places where people can talk about the issue of homosexuality in a helpful and respectful manner.

Given our goal, the tone of this book is pastoral, not doctrinaire. In fact, for many months the book had the working title "A Safe Place to Talk about Homosexuality." We recognized that a lot of people feel afraid when they talk about homosexuality, and we wanted to demonstrate that people at every point on the spectrum of opinion can feel "safe" when dealing with the topic—that everyone can be heard and treated with respect. We also wanted to show that people can have honest differences of opinion about important matters—that those with whom we disagree are neither radicals nor reactionaries. There are many kinds of individuals and churches. Some easily welcome folks who are different, some do not, and most are in the middle. But the congregation ought to be a place where all people are welcome to engage in their own struggle.

The intended audience for this book is pastors and lay leaders who are thinking about developing a plan to guide members and friends of their congregation in a study of homosexuality. Thus, the focus of this book is less on the content of the discussion than on the process. Four foundational chapters will help planners form a big-picture understanding of what they are undertaking. In chapter 1, Sylvia Thorson-Smith summarizes the history of the church's teaching about sexuality in general and concisely defines three dualisms that tend to color all our thinking about sexuality. Karen McClintock narrows the picture in chapter 2 when she offers a theory about why—on an emotional level—homosexuality is hard for many of us to talk about. Carl Dudley and Hugh Halverstadt suggest in chapter 3 that because passions often run high when the topic of homosexuality arises, the issue requires special handling. And in chapter 4, Marc Kolden lays out ten rules for talking about difficult issues and applies the rules to discussing homosexuality.

Part 2 consists of seven case studies from congregations that have undertaken a formal study of homosexuality. We made use of case studies because we believe they will enable congregations to learn from the experience of those who have gone before them. We chose the contributing churches from among about 20 we interviewed, selecting those we thought had the most to teach—because they devised a unique and successful strategy or dealt with significant pain. Four of the churches are United Church of Christ. This is not too surprising, considering that the denomination voted in 1985 to encourage congregations to "adopt a non-discrimination policy and a Covenant of Openness and Affirmation of persons of lesbian, gay, and bisexual orientation within the community of faith."[2] Through this resolution, UCC congregations were given a real push to talk about homosexuality and are therefore considered by some church leaders to be "out in front" in their ability to do this well.

When we invited the congregations (usually through the pastor but sometimes a lay leader) to tell their story, we asked them to tell us why they decided to talk about homosexuality, how they went about conducting their study and conversation, what they learned from the experience, what they wished they had done differently, and how the congregation changed as a result of the conversation. We also reminded the contributors they were not writing for "Lives of the Saints," that their congregation would be a resource for others who are considering study and conversation about homosexuality, and that therefore our readers need to hear what their experience was really like, with its ups and downs, joy and pain, successes and regrets.

As readers move from part 1 to part 2 of the book, they will discover one of the basic principles at work in this volume: We did not try to force our contributors to agree with one another! At the end of part 1, Kolden argues, for example, that congregations that want to talk about homosexuality should not hang over participants' heads the threat of some kind of vote. And yet all seven of the churches in our case studies did have just such a vote. Readers may decide for themselves whether this was wise. Readers might also notice that some contributors talk about gays and lesbians; some refer to gays, lesbians, and bisexuals; and others add transgendered people to the list of those discussed. We discovered when preparing this book that there is disagreement even within the homosexual community about what exactly "homosexual" means. So we let stand each contributor's assumptions about the matter.

Some readers will not be familiar with the various parachurch organizations mentioned in the case studies. As noted above, it was in the 1970s that mainline congregations across the United States began discussing issues related to homosexuality. Beginning in 1983, organizations have formed in ten denominations as grassroots efforts to bring about change in their denominations' attitudes, teachings, and policies regarding homosexuality, and to support participating congregations' and other groups' (such as campus ministries and judicatories) intentions to be welcoming to gays and lesbians. These organizations, listed in the resource section at the end of this book, refer to themselves as "the welcoming movement." (Also associated with most mainline denominations is another group of organizations: gay/lesbian/bisexual coalitions and caucuses, such as the United Church Coalition for Lesbian/Gay Concerns, Lutherans Concerned/North America, and Interweave (UUA). Names and addresses for these groups have not been included in the resource list but can easily be obtained from the welcoming program offices.) The various welcoming programs generally are able to suggest study materials, provide resource lists, and propose ways congregations might structure their conversation.

Certainly there are other kinds of congregations and organizations and other processes from which churches could learn. But we believe the seven case studies in this book will provide readers with many useful ideas for their own congregations. We also think they will find particularly instructive the case study analyses in part 3, provided by Donald Bossart and Speed Leas, two writers with considerable experience dealing with issues of conflict and community. Through their observations, readers have the opportunity, as they did in part 1, to devise principles to guide a congregation's study process.

The subtitle of this book is *Dialogue on a Difficult Issue*. The word *dialogue* comes from two Greek words, *dia*, "across," and *legein*, "to speak." Of course, dialogue requires not just speaking but listening. And teacher and author Ronald Heifetz observes, "Listening is a trial-and-error process of making an interpretation, seeing where it falls short, and revising it. To listen, one has to live with doubt."[3] It is our hope that congregational leaders will find in this book the guidance they need to create a space where helpful, respectful dialogue on homosexuality can take place. Readers will know they have succeeded in defining such a space when dialogue participants feel confident that their church is a safe place to speak as well as a place where they can safely live with the doubt required of listening. Then readers will know what it means to engage in true dialogue on this difficult issue.

ACKNOWLEDGMENTS

The resource list was compiled with the assistance of Janelle Bussert, assistant professor of religion, Augsburg College, Minneapolis, Minnesota; Ralph Carter, Rochester, New York, who prepares a list of resources for The More Light Churches Network; and Ann B. Day, Holden, Massachusetts, coordinator of the Open and Affirming Program. These people also provided valuable background information and other assistance throughout this project, as did Mark Bowman, Chicago, Illinois, coordinator of the Reconciling Congregation Program; Dick Lundy, Wayzata, Minnesota, co-coordinator of The More Light Churches Network; and David Lott, Saint Paul, Minnesota, friend and Fortress Press editor of Augsburg Fortress, Publishers.

PART 1

Getting Ready to Talk

CHAPTER 1

Talking about Sexuality

Sylvia Thorson-Smith

Ethicist Marvin M. Ellison begins the introduction to his book *Erotic Justice* by observing that "everywhere in this culture people realize that sexuality and family life are in crisis, but no consensus exists about the nature of the problem or its solution." Having identified this reality, Ellison suggests that "we need moral discourse that can confront the depth of this cultural crisis and also appreciate how justice, as communally secured respect and regard for persons, is foundational to good loving."[1]

Such discourse is very difficult to have in the church. Talking about sexuality and engaging in deep moral reflection about the sexual dimension of our lives is off-limits for many Christians. We soon discover, if we choose to take the risk, that dialogue in congregational settings about our communal understanding of sexual love and justice is a particularly difficult undertaking.

Marvin Ellison and I know well the challenge of talking about sexuality in church. From 1988-1991, we served together on the 17-member General Assembly Committee on Human Sexuality for the Presbyterian Church (U.S.A.). It was the task of our committee to study the broad range of sexuality issues and prepare a report and recommendations for our denomination. Our work resulted in a highly publicized and controversial report, "Keeping Body and Soul Together: Sexuality, Spirituality, and Social Justice," and we discovered that efforts to talk about sexuality expose not only the differences among us but the complex relationship between sexuality and spirituality in Christian history.

One experience in preparing this report stands out as a vivid illustration of the conflicted response that accompanies discussions of sexuality in church. Our committee met in cities across the country and had conversations with many adult Sunday school classes to identify issues about human sexuality that affect individuals directly. During one particular visit, class members revealed very little about their personal lives and issues affecting them, speaking primarily in the abstract about homosexuality as sin but without any firsthand knowledge of lesbians or gay men. Asked repeatedly about sexuality issues affecting their own lives, no one responded. Following the session, however, one person in the class approached a member of our committee and revealed that she was a brokenhearted parent, unable to talk with her own daughter about sexual decisions and finding no help from her pastor and her church to bridge the communication gap. Furthermore, she noted that several others in the class, who had said nothing, were rearing their grandchildren, alienated from their own adult children and confused about cultural changes in sexual attitudes and behaviors that intimately affected their own lives. Their silence in the church school class, however, was deafening.

We live in the midst of a cultural crisis involving sexuality. Changes in family patterns, sexual relationships, gender arrangements, the meaning of sexual orientation and identity, media images, medical developments involving reproduction, awareness of sexual violence and abuse, the prevalence of sexually transmitted diseases, and the social response to HIV/AIDS all reflect cultural conflict and challenge to established norms. We are surrounded by all kinds of messages about the body and sexuality, but at church we participate in a pervasive, collective silence about these very issues. Our culture bombards us with talk about sex; our churches say little or nothing.

Every week, we sit in pews and quietly hide the truth of our lives from one another: his son is gay; she is a survivor of sexual abuse; their marriage is coming apart; she does not know what to do about an unwanted pregnancy; she is in a loving lesbian relationship and does not say anything about her partner to her church friends. Every week we greet each other warmly, worship God together, and mask important aspects of who we really are and what we would most like to say to each other. Why do we feel so reticent to reveal the sexual elements of our identity when we are gathered together as a church community? And why is it that the church is such an uncomfortable place to talk about the sexual issues that are central to the fabric of our lives?

The Historical Legacy

We have considerable baggage to unpack when we attempt to talk about
sexuality in church. Examining the history of Christianity reveals deep
ambivalence toward the body and sexuality as well as conflicted beliefs
about the relationship between sexuality and spirituality. It is this historical legacy that we must explore if we are to understand why talking
about sexuality is such a challenge in our day.

Sexuality as described in the Bible and in Christian tradition re-
flects a dualistic framework for constructing sexual and gender arrangements. Such dualistic thinking is present in Christian assumptions that
sexuality is fundamentally antagonistic to spirituality. In a variety of
biblical texts and writings by early teachers of the church, we find evidence that sexuality was regarded with deep suspicion, that the body's
erotic desires were seen as dangerous temptations to sin, and that the
ideal spiritual pursuit included control, denial, and suppression of bodily
passion and sexual expression. For many Christians, turning toward God
has meant turning away from the body and sexuality.

This dualistic tradition regarding sexuality has been manifested in
at least three specific and enduring conflicts.

Tension between Things Sexual and Things Spiritual

We are the inheritors of a religious tradition that has instilled in each
of us some measure of distrust for our bodies and our sexuality. The
notion that flesh and spirit are separate, with spiritual matters elevated
over corporeal matters, pervades our theological heritage. Putting aside
concerns of "the flesh" (in other words, the body) to attend to concerns
of the spirit is often seen as a demonstration of the highest pursuit of
Christian life. Because our body, and hence our sexuality, is the center
of our occasion for sin, death, and fallenness, our faithfulness as Christian disciples is tested by our control over this potentially unbridled
locus for evil. Little wonder that we regard talk about sexuality in
church as dangerous, when we have learned well that everything sexual
is fraught with danger and jeopardizes our calling as spiritual people.

Tensions between Men and Women

The opposition of sexuality and spirituality in Christian theology has
been accompanied by a dimension of gender dualism as well. From
Hebrew texts that caution men about the impurities of women's bodies
and the potentially evil purposes of female sexuality to New Testament
texts that suggest women are subordinate to men by the order of creation, we can see that both Judaism and Christianity were established as
patriarchal institutions according to a hierarchy of male authority and
dominance. That women are created inferior to men in their bodies and
their sexuality, if not in their spirits, has been a central tenet of most of
Christendom until this century, when movements for women's equality
have included rethinking traditional gender arrangements in the church.
The history of Christianity, however, is primarily a record of male clerics
and theologians whose ideas about sexuality rest, in large measure, on
the control of women, women's bodies, and women's sexuality.

Perpetuation of this gender dualism has had serious repercussions
for men and male sexuality as well. When anything sensual, erotic, and
earthy is associated with females and "the feminine," men not only regard women as dangerously different but see all such desires within
themselves as suggestive that they might not be "real" men. Homophobia (the fear of homosexuality) has a disproportionate grip on the lives
and psyches of men, in large part because the fear of homosexuality is
closely associated with the fear of being womanly, less than fully mascu-
line. When maleness is accorded greater status and power in virtually all
social hierarchies, is it any wonder that men fear the loss of such privilege by anything that would feminize or emasculate them in the eyes of
others?

Tensions between the Public and the Private

This third dualism has a particularly pernicious hold on the church and
constitutes much of the reason why it is so hard to talk about sexuality.
The opposition of public to private can be traced to the 19th century
idea that work took place in the public sphere, and family and leisure
were relegated to the private sphere of the home. The rise of American
industry took labor to the site of business and factory, disconnecting it

from rural communities where home, family, work, and gender roles commingled. These social changes also had profound implications for religious institutions. Women in the dominant, white cultural ideal were seen as "keepers of the home," guardians of the nobler virtues of care, compassion, and spiritual devotion, and the church (as an increasingly feminized institution) became regarded as a site for religious, but not worldly, matters. People went to church to feel spiritual, not to be engaged by issues of society. The late 19th century also gave rise to church-related initiatives for social justice; however, the past 100 years have been marked by a persistent religious sentiment that church is a place for nurturing life in the spirit, separate from life in its social-political dimensions.

This increasingly rigid separation of the public from the private along lines of work and family was accompanied by new attitudes about sexuality. Matters regarding sex were sequestered behind closed doors, hidden from the world (including the church), and relegated to the dark recesses of home and private life. What Christians did sexually was regarded as intensely private, and the public exposure of one's sexual activity invited disapproval. Women could barely go out in public if they were pregnant, obviously announcing by their condition that they had engaged in sex. (In the case of ministers' wives, this evidence was particularly disturbing to see!) No matter whether the issue was sexual relations between spouses, sexual abuse, same-sex relationships, or re-productive issues, topics pertaining to sexuality were not fit for discussion in "polite," or public, company. In keeping with these developments, the church itself became the primary sanctuary of polite company.

Two dualistic oppositions influencing Christian thought and experience—between sexuality and spirituality, and between men and women—were joined now by this third antagonism, between public and private, to secure a powerful base of resistance to talking about sexuality in church. Perhaps a minister might preach about the well-known but little-discussed rules for sexual behavior, but would he invite members to talk with each other about the full implications of sexuality in their lives? No way. That development did not take place until recently.

Before leaving this historical discussion, it is important to note that although this dualistic framework has dominated Christian theology and experience, it does not reflect the entire picture. In his book *Body Theology*, James B. Nelson, a leading voice in unpacking the sexual baggage of church history, answers the question "Where are we?" by identifying both the "sinful problems" and the "virtuous possibilities" in Christian tradition that give the church particular power for doing both good and ill on matters related to sexuality.[2] Not only do we approach discussions of sexuality with the baggage of our dualistic past, but we also carry with us some mightily constructive sources for rethinking sexuality. As Christians we are people of the Incarnation who affirm as central to our beliefs that:

- God created the world and all flesh good;
- women as well as men are created in the image and likeness of God;
- God so loved the world that God's very self became flesh;
- every person is a child of God who is to be valued and included in the human, and especially the Christian, community;
- we are created to love each other just as we love our own embodied selves;
- we are called to break the yokes that oppress people and free them for lives of joy and relationship.

Such convictions are our strength for wrestling with the most difficult issues of sexuality. We do it best by confronting the complexity of our history and searching our tradition for examples of courage to engage in this important undertaking. We also do it best with a deep sense of humility as we recognize that we are surrounded by a "cloud of witnesses" who sought to be faithful in different times and places. We, too, seek to be faithful Christian disciples as we talk about human sexuality today.

Good News/Bad News

When talking about sexuality with church groups during the past decade, I have discovered that these conversations are greeted as "good news" by many people and are also seen as very unwelcome, "bad news" experiences by many other people. When we released the human sexuality report to the Presbyterian Church in 1991, it was greeted with deep appreciation by those who were eager to talk about sexuality and open up the dialogue about sexuality issues, but it was also met with hostility by those who had no desire to examine human sexuality in any way that would alter their firmly held opinions. In particular, resistance was most intense to discussions that included consideration of Christian standards for same-sex relationships and nonmarital heterosexual relationships.

Talking about sexuality involves a willingness to share and try to understand what it is like to live outside the bounds of privilege as well as what it is like to examine and perhaps relinquish one's privilege. Just talking with one another does not guarantee a particular result; however, conversations about sexuality among people of good will do open the way for something new to happen in the encounter. To talk about sexuality is to engage in truth telling. Congregations that provide opportunities to talk about sexuality invite heterosexuals and nonheterosexuals alike to explore truthfully the challenges we face when living faithful Christian lives. To meet each other truthfully in the search for wholeness as sexual-spiritual beings can give birth to gracious, justice-loving community.

Justice … Kindness … Humility

Talking about sexuality in the church means engaging in the search for a relevant Christian sexual ethic for our day. Church struggles over sexuality seem to focus disproportionately on the issues of homosexuality and the status of lesbians and gay men in our denominations. As long as these faith communities accord such privileges as ordination and the blessing of covenantal relationships to heterosexuals only, justice demands that these issues remain top priorities in our conversations together.

Issues of homosexuality are actually only one aspect of the much broader topic of human sexuality, however. Christians today are wrestling with their understanding of all ethical questions surrounding sexual relationships and are examining whether any nonheterosexual or nonmarital sexual relations can be consistent with Christian discipleship. Many denominations are engaged in intense struggles over passage of ordination standards that would only allow sex in marriage between a man and a woman, and celibacy in singleness. Some are considering alternative language such as "fidelity and integrity" in relationships, still maintaining the importance of sexual standards while recognizing that many same-sex or nonmarital relationships are authentically Christian and should not be obstacles to leadership and blessings of the church.

We might ask, then, what is our authority for exploring a new framework for sexual ethics that could include relationships other than heterosexual marriage only? And what might be the marks of Christian sexual relationship for people of all sexual orientations? If we are willing to ask these questions and engage in dialogue about our responses to them, it is because we believe we must take seriously the biblical injunction in Micah 6:8: to do justice, to love kindness, and to walk humbly with our God.

Doing justice on matters of human sexuality means attending to fairness, mutual regard, and sharing of power and privileges equally. It means being willing to listen to the truth of others as much as sharing our own truth. It involves risk taking on behalf of the "other" who is disadvantaged, powerless, the outsider, or the marginal. We need to be justice seekers and justice doers, in our own intimate relationships and in our communal ordering of sexuality as well.

Loving kindness puts us to the test when we are asked to talk about sexuality. It may mean that we reconsider whom we say we love and how we love them. I have heard many church members profess the Christian mandate of love for all people, but such a profession sounds very abstract when they do not know any gay people, are unwilling to encounter gay people, and would prefer that gay people not talk about who they are. It seems that a simple test of whether we are really loving lesbians, gay men, bisexual, and transgendered persons (or anyone, for that matter) should be whether or not they *feel* loved by us. People know what love feels like; many people of different sexual orientations and experiences are not feeling loved by Christians and our denominational policies regarding them. They are feeling excluded, isolated, silenced, even abused. When we love kindness and relate to one another in love and justice, we reach out across all barriers and encounter each other in radical, risk-taking acts of mutual relationship.

Walking humbly is, in many ways, the hardest test of all when we are talking about sexuality. There is so much we think we know and so much to fear if we admit to our uncertainties. The more I study human sexuality, the more I recognize what a mystery it is. Proverbs 30:18-19 identifies four things "that are too mysterious" to understand, including a man and a woman falling in love. Popular songs echo, "Who can explain it, who can tell you why?" Today we are also challenged to talk about the mystery of same-sex love, which requires the same humility in the presence of mystery that was described by the biblical writer of the proverb. Walking with God as we talk about sexuality invites us into a deeper experience of humility, where grace and understanding may be made known to us in the testimony of each other's lives.

> God, you are always in our future,
> beckoning us toward a horizon
> we are not sure we want to reach.
> We think of the things that are past
> and wish you would give us, again,
> that with which we were comfortable.
> But you lead us from the future.
> Thank you for the assurance
> that we will not be without you then,
> as we are not without you now,
> and give us the courage
> to follow your lead.
> —James Richards[3]

Talking about sexuality in church is not easy. It is hard work, and we should expect to move out of our comfort zones into unfamiliar places. We commit ourselves to these conversations in the hope that we will encounter each other in more meaningful ways and deepen our own experience of faith and community. We also trust that God is leading us, and our assurance of God's presence in the struggle sustains us for the difficulties we face. Through it all, we believe that faithfulness to the Gospel calls us to new life, including new life in our sexuality and all our relationships. Talking about sexuality can be unexpectedly, even joyfully, good news!

CHAPTER 2

Why Is Homosexuality So Hard to Talk About?

Karen A. McClintock

When author and theologian Will Campbell was asked, "Will the church ever get comfortable with homosexuality?" he replied, "The institutional church has never come to grips with heterosexuality."[1] Sexuality is a hard topic to talk about. Our identities are uniquely wrapped up in our experiences and feelings as sexual people. Our choice of partners, how we express ourselves with our bodies, and the power and sacredness of sexual intercourse shape the very core of our being. We have touted the virtues of healthy sexuality and decried its abuse. We have heard sexual union described simultaneously as "heaven" and the "road to hell."

Discussions of homosexuality are often influenced by years of learning about how we are to respond to those who deviate from the sexual "norm." Against this learned background, church leaders, recognizing the need for value-centered conversations on homosexuality, have urged congregations into dialogue. Retired United Methodist Bishop Leontine Kelly, an outspoken advocate of human and civil rights observed, "There is nothing in life that cannot be talked about [in the church]."[2]

Unfortunately, this has not historically been the case. As frightened as we are of all eroticism, we are even more frightened of homoerotic attraction. Discussions about the emotional and physical aspects of human sexuality in general have been few and far between and generally difficult when they have occurred.

Up until 1968, the American Psychiatric Association listed homosexuality as a deviant behavior, along with mental disorders such as schizophrenia and chronic depression.[3] The past 20 years have seen a tremendous change in thinking about homosexual inclination and activity. The psychiatric community today considers homosexuality to be both biologically and culturally based. With new scientific evidence for the given nature of sexual orientation, the counseling community, the church—indeed, our whole society—is challenged to examine our assumptions.

Nonetheless, leaders who choose to discuss homosexuality, particularly the inclusion of gay men and lesbians in the life of a congregation, find themselves up against the "don't talk, don't feel" taboos many individuals learn within family systems. Almost every extended family has at least one gay, lesbian, or bisexual member. This family member may be acknowledged only sometimes—and may often be whispered or laughed about, denied recognition, or shunned. During discussions on the involvement of self-avowed homosexuals in the church, there will be people present for whom the subject is deeply personal, because they themselves are homosexual or because a family member or close friend is. Because people do have these personal, though secret, connections with someone who is homosexual, layers of defensive emotions, internal and external, will likely rise to the surface when people dare to begin talking about homosexuality.

In preparation for any discussions about homosexuality, laity and clergy alike need to be sensitive to their own opinions and feelings, and well informed of the stages individuals and congregations go through as they engage in conversation. They need to recognize that cultural shame once kept many individuals bound in secrecy, but today people are speaking more boldly.

In and Out of the Closet

The process of acknowledging and disclosing one's gay, lesbian, or bisexual orientation is commonly called "coming out of the closet." This closet of silence has been a closet of safety for gay men and lesbians in the church and the community. Its darkness provides a cover that keeps out prejudice and hatred. Threatened with the loss of community, respect, and lifelong friends, one can understand the benefits of silence. Because coming out of the closet means losing these benefits, the process can be frightening and painful.

But the closet has been more than a place of privacy; it has been a place of secrecy, where shame and betrayal have eroded human dignity and left untold scars on individuals and congregations. In the closet, the pain of being different is borne in silence. I know this personally, because my father, who was gay, lived and died at a time when the closet was his only option. My mother and he remained married, and to the outside world we looked like any other good Christian family. But we shared this deeply embarrassing secret. My parents had taken vows of silence. My father was gay.

Our family was surrounded by an unconscious cloud of shame. Mother was silently loyal although deeply unfulfilled. My sister and I learned as children to live with and recreate environments characterized by secrets and shame. Our church, like most congregations in the '50s and '60s, was alive with growth. As a child I learned of God's love for all people including my family. But I also grew to understand that talking about sexuality in church was taboo. The congregation's silence unwittingly contributed to the isolation and darkness of the family secret.

My own coming-out process as the daughter of a gay father included a need to reconcile the reality of his sexual orientation with my Christian values. The Scriptures had taught me to honor my father and my mother. But every Sunday afternoon, my uncle brought tracts to inform our family about right beliefs and to warn us about the "sin of homosexuality." My internal identity had already been unconsciously shaped by my father's unspoken gay identity—and my uncle's hatred. The integration of my faith and my acceptance of my father's sexual orientation took me through a process not unlike the coming-out process for gay men, lesbians, and bisexuals. As I can personally attest, coming out is very hard work.

My first task was to accept my parents' decision to remain secretive. The intense judgement that our culture has shown toward homosexuals had affected us all. My father's sense of unworthiness about his sexuality was reinforced in the military, in his studies in psychology, and in the church. Children internalize the identity of each parent at an early age. Any judgment on the part of others toward the parent's behavior or beliefs is experienced by the child as judgment that affects self-esteem. I am particularly concerned that congregations that open discussions on homosexuality be mindful of the children. Youth or children who have homosexual parents and who overhear comments about their parents being "immoral," "shameful," or "sinful" will easily internalize those judgments and apply them to themselves. These young people will grow up with a profound sense of shame, increased anxiety, and lower self-esteem. Great care is required to avoid adding to the sense of shame already present in the lives of gay men, lesbians, bisexuals, and transgendered individuals and their families.

Congregations Coming Out

As was discussed more thoroughly in the previous chapter, many Christians have great difficulty talking about sexuality in general. Individuals' fear and shame often make homosexuality in particular even more difficult to discuss. When congregations begin talking about homosexuality, they need to be aware that they may engage in a process that in many ways parallels the process individuals go through when they come out of the closet. The process involves a careful reflection on spiritual as well as emotional experiences and beliefs. The search for personal or community wholeness is a courageous process that often feels like walking through dangerous territory. And just as it can be difficult for individuals to come out of the closet, it can be painful for congregations to do the reflecting and searching that is required.

Many churches are now discussing homosexuality, not without pain, but they are doing so nevertheless. Dialogues have been initiated by individuals who have disclosed their sexual orientation and by family members who need to tell about the painfulness of their family secrets. It should not surprise us that the church "family" would be transformed when loving communication takes place. Homosexuals, their family members, and friends who are coming out of their closets—people whose faces are recognizable to members of the church—are asking their communities of faith to do the same.

Individuals coming out of the closet go through a multistage process of self-acceptance and integration according to Vivienne Cass of the Department of Psychology, University of Western Australia, Nedlands. Dr. Cass's six-stage model includes identity confusion, identity comparison, identity tolerance, identity acceptance, identity pride, and identity synthesis.[4] Borrowing from Dr. Cass's model, I propose that a similar multistage process happens in churches emerging from silence and struggling to embrace new perspectives. Understanding these stages can assist leaders and pastors in reducing fear, minimizing conflict, protecting the sense of sacred worth that each individual needs to experience the love of God—and appreciating why it is so hard to talk about homosexuality.

I recognize not all congregations that discuss the issue will continue through all stages of this process and reach a certain conclusion. Those that move through the process and adopt a position in favor of the full inclusion of homosexuals in the life of the church, however, will find they are likely to experience all these stages.

Stage One: Confusion

In most congregations, the decision to talk about members' stance toward gay and lesbian people begins with one individual's confession. This may be a gay or lesbian person or a family member.

Sitting with Ralph and Marilyn in their family home after their son's funeral service, we shared long silences. Their son had died of AIDS, and they wanted to talk in confidence with their pastor. Ralph was angry and confused. Marilyn sighed with deep incomprehension. Their religious training had taught them to hate the "sin" of their son's homosexuality, and yet they loved him. They bore the pain of his death in silence for many years until a young man in their church fellowship announced that he was HIV-positive. At prayer time the next Sunday morning, they told their family secret to the church. It opened the congregation's heart and the discussions began. But in the early first stage of the process, the church was as confused as Ralph and Marilyn had been.

In the church, as in nuclear families, the system is shaken by the disclosure that a member of the system is a homosexual. Denial, accompanied by anger and fear, is often the first response. The overall desire of the system is to go back to its former equilibrium. Peter L. Steinke, in his book *Healthy Congregations: A Systems Approach*, writes, "Change in one part produces change in another part, even in the whole. There is a 'ripple' through the system."[5] Nearly always, the system resists.

Centuries-old biblical and theological views and issues surface. Although the Levitical tradition includes homosexual cult prostitution in a long list of prohibitions, Jesus was silent on the subject. A plethora of interpretations about these teachings can heighten conflict in this stage of confusion.

When discussions surface about homosexuality, some practical and organizational issues arise. The church has long identified itself as being for heterosexuals only—through mailing lists, couples' groups, and family activities. People feel unsure about what to say to children and youth concerning homosexuality. Debates about holy unions are bound to intensify disagreements. The fear arises and may be expressed that talking about homosexuality will be interpreted as promoting it. When an individual says to the church, "We have to talk about this," this often introduces time Cass describes as "confusion and turmoil."[6] This is a period of alienation, fear, and resistance.

Some congregations experience what Cass calls "internalized homophobia." At the heart of the corporate fear will be found an individual who fears his or her own homosexuality. This person, who would never come out of the closet, will sometimes resist any discussion of homosexuality. The resistance of the individual can in turn affect the whole church. This person's moral stance has been described by Cass and others as the "Moral Crusader."[7] Most congregations have one or more of these people, who rise to the surface when homosexuality is discussed publicly. Moral Crusaders attempt to return the congregation to its former state of silence, lessening the discomfort of confusion and conflict within themselves and the church. These people are not simply holding a different opinion, as some congregants will do; they are resisting the conversation due to inner pain and turmoil. These people deserve to be listened to in the same compassionate and nondefensive manner as the gay, lesbian, or bisexual person.

Congregations at this stage may focus on the distinction between homosexual behavior and identity. Denominational mandates that single clergy be celibate clearly differentiate between the desire and the act. "They can join our church, if they are not acting on their tendencies." "We can love your daughter but not her behavior." These arguments allow those who feel uncomfortable to focus on individuals as "problems" rather than to struggle with what it means to love the homosexual "neighbor."

The healing step in phase one is to embrace the inevitable ambiguity, discomfort, and confusion as normal. In this phase the task for leaders is to keep the discussion open. As William Sloane Coffin once said, "You can live with ambiguity, if you are a person of faith."[8]

Stage Two: Comparison

A congregation at stage two has accepted the reality that it has within it homosexual and bisexual people and their loved ones. Diversity is recognized and named. Task forces, discussion groups, guest speakers are called on to facilitate communication.

At this point in the discussion, people are listening for the opinions of other trusted members and leaders of the congregation. Ideas are weighed and compared with long-held positions.

As the discussion broadens, individuals who have disclosed their homosexuality may feel more alienated. If the discussion is framed in terms of morality, participants may unknowingly wound the disclosing individuals. The conversation at this stage needs to be based on personal story and experience rather than biblical or theological rhetoric. This allows each participant to move into a deeper level of trust and to begin taking the risk of telling his or her life story. Speaking about sexuality with a loved one is difficult, and it is even more difficult to talk with a group or community. Disclosure requires a feeling of utmost safety. If the conversation is managed from an intellectual perspective only, participants are less likely to name the experiences upon which their opinions are formed.

When "Fred" learned that his new pastor had last served an Open and Affirming church, he was not sure what to do. Fred had never healed from an incident of his youth when two of his friends tried to coerce him into a sexual threesome. Rather than get help to understand and free himself from the shame he felt about that incident, Fred turned his humiliation, fear, anger, and hatred against the entire homosexual community. He felt that if his church accepted homosexuals, it betrayed him. He sabotaged the church's communication process by going to his coworkers and friends in the community to talk about his opinions. He had to contrast his views with those of church members who were openly accepting of gays, lesbians, and bisexuals, in order to honor his own pain.

In this stage, not only the individual, but the congregation as a whole begins to express concern for its reputation in the community. Laity and clergy may try to assess the outcome of a conversation by discussing the matter with colleagues. Just as an individual seeks support groups for gays or lesbians or their loved ones, the church moving toward a more public statement on this issue will begin to explore identification with like-minded congregations.[9]

The congregation may try to recover its mission of justice with statements such as, "We understand ourselves to be different." "We understand our stance to be modeled on the ministry of Jesus." And "Our decision is a positive reflection of our beliefs." Whether or not the congregation closes dialogue at this stage, the church will be comparing itself to other congregations in its community and denomination. In this way, a unique identity is sought.

In the homosexual community people talk about "passing." This is the way a homosexual portrays himself or herself as heterosexual to avoid the scrutiny of others whose prejudicial treatment could result in the loss of a job, insurance, housing, or other benefits afforded the heterosexual community. By keeping silent about his or her homosexuality, the person passes as a heterosexual. Congregations engaging in passing strategies may try to silence discussions, control the materials people read and the people who speak, or use denominational "rules" as reasons to delay the process of open discussion. By keeping silent, these congregations hide their openness to homosexuals and pass as heterosexually oriented.

When Sue and Jan began to be strong leaders of a small suburban church, they were clear with the pastor about their homosexuality. With her encouragement, they picked a time at a leadership meeting to talk with those assembled about their upcoming wedding anniversary. The response was warm and caring. Sue taught Sunday school and Jan chaired the board for two years. During this time, they continued to ask their pastor and key lay leaders to engage in a process of dialogue toward becoming a Reconciling Congregation.[10] In spite of the church's acceptance of Sue and Jan, their requests were largely ignored. Sue and Jan perceived that the church was, in fact, "passing": trying to be open to individuals without facing a transformation process and disclosing to the community that they were a place of welcome to homosexuals.

Gay and lesbian members can expect to experience acute alienation at this stage. A lesbian couple seeking a service of holy union in the church where they had been active and openly homosexual for several years were told by their pastor that he could not perform the ceremony in the sanctuary. The pastor was afraid significant donors would leave and that the bishop would not allow it. When the couple compared their own beliefs and values with the church's mixed messages they felt betrayed.

Stage Three: Tolerance

If a congregation continues to move toward acceptance and inclusion of gays, lesbians, and bisexuals, they will continue through the coming-out stages. At stage three, a significant shift takes place for individuals and congregations: the realignment of relationships. Earlier stages of turmoil and confusion are reduced, and the congregation seeks greater congruency between inward feelings and beliefs and outward presentation. Although this stage appears to be more peaceful than the first two, it still involves hard work.

Many congregations in this process present written materials for discussion. Mission statements, or statements of open affirmation of all people, are tested and revised. Even in this time of increasing tolerance, care should be taken to avoid polarizing votes. When a United Methodist church in the San Francisco Bay area recently became a Reconciling Congregation, the board decided by two votes to make a public statement of welcome. With so little consensus, tolerance actually decreased rather than increasing. A delayed vote, with further discussion and time for integration, might have resulted in a more cohesive position.

All change and transformation involves gains and losses. The goal is to maximize gains and minimize losses. If a congregation adopts a new identity as an Open and Affirming church, those who do not believe this state to be consistent with moral and biblical values will withdraw. Some gay, lesbian, and bisexual people who remain closeted may also leave the parish. Strategies to release members with love need to be discussed and provided. Leaders who can envision the gains beyond the current losses will help their congregations through a time of grief and into the next stages. Anytime a congregation more closely defines its mission and ministry, growth is likely to occur.

Stage Four: Acceptance

In the church that continues to this stage of the coming-out process, a new set of associations probably will occur. Sometimes in tension with denominational positions, leaders form alliances among Open and Affirming congregations.[11] These new associations strengthen the congregation's sense of self-pride. The church might seek ways to express its new position through compassionate ministries within the homosexual community, working for justice in housing and employment, or serving those living with HIV or AIDS. The congregation as a whole shifts away from previously defined norms, welcoming new members from the gay/lesbian/bisexual community and new members who have loved ones in that community.

Stage Five: Pride

When a new pastor arrived at her parish in San Francisco, church leaders invited her to participate in the gay pride parade. The congregation's identity was shaped by its ministry with and for homosexuals in the neighborhood. Members provided healing services for the loved ones of those who died of AIDS, participated in the quilt project commemorating loved ones lost, and offered grief and loss support groups. This congregation felt a deep sense of pride in members' love of one another and their mission.

When a church feels proud of its identity, a deep sense of joy emerges. Language changes begin to reflect the actual diversity of the membership. The term "partner" is used to describe a committed loved one. The bulletin includes a variety of activities that meet the needs of the entire congregation. The anniversaries of gay men and lesbians are noted and celebrated.

At this stage, the church's self-acceptance develops despite the possibilities of society's rejection. Seeking justice for the community becomes a stronger core value than the protection of individual comfort. Family members depend on the church to join them in the fight for civil rights in housing and employment. The church that supports these family members watches healing take place after years of alienation.

Stage Six: Synthesis

The church may feel itself wrapped in this coming-out process for a long period of time. But when the inner acceptance and the public image become clear, the issue recedes and the church feels that its openness is just one aspect of its fuller identity as the body of Christ.

Individuals on both sides of these debates offer reconciliation in order to move forward. Lay leaders and clergy will need to offer signs of peace in worship, committee life, and communications. When congregations break through long-standing taboos that say it is wrong to discuss sexuality in the church, they pave the way for healing. They make it possible to reach Bishop Kelly's dream that we be a church that can discuss anything and everything. The church that has come out of the closet has left behind its own secrets and its own darkness, and with courage steps forth to welcome others.

Traditions, beliefs, fears, and long-standing taboos make it impossible for many church members to come out of the closet. When a member makes a disclosure about himself or herself or about a family member, the resulting turmoil may eventually lead to a joyful, growth-filled congregation. This concluding stage shows that the coming-out process can evolve into a compassionate love for self and others. In this final stage, the individual and congregation at last experience a time of great hope and satisfaction.

Conclusion

On national coming out day I told the board of a parish I was serving that I had an announcement to make "in honor of national coming out day." In that moment, I experienced the terror that must have kept my father, and many others, in silence. The fear in the room was palpable. When I told them that my father was gay, they offered a corporate sigh of relief. The tension eased.

I used the moment to invite them into open discussion. Compelled by culture and responsive to loved ones, the church will be called on more and more often to discuss sexuality, and particularly homosexuality. Each person's story and faith journey are deeply connected to his or her sexuality.

And so we talk about it. We talk about it for our fathers, some of whom live in shame and await a word of grace. We talk about it for our children, some of whom come seeking a church where their sexuality is affirmed. We talk about it for ourselves, for many of us have unresolved and complicated feelings on this issue. We talk about it for the witness of the church in each community. My witness is presented here with the goal that our dialogues be grounded in the love of God and blessed by the healing compassion of the Holy Spirit.

CHAPTER 3

Explosive Issues Require Special Handling

Carl S. Dudley and Hugh F. Halverstadt

Extraordinary Conflicts

In every generation, sometimes every decade, society faces issues that are too hot to handle and must be treated in unique ways. Because these issues challenge common assumptions and threaten the status quo, many people who are comfortable with their place in the established order will go to great lengths, even suspend normal rules of human relations and moral decency, to resist change and retain the old world. In these extraordinary tensions between possible change and intractable resistance, language is misunderstood, motives are vilified, and innocent activities are perceived as evil and threatening.

These conditions are so socially explosive that they set off the same emotional conditions as being at war, and radical elements will even feel justified to commit murder in the name of their cause. In this century, we have seen this level of irrational hostility surrounding several issues, such as organizing labor unions, granting women the right to vote, recognizing civil rights for people of color, and allowing women to obtain an abortion. Welcoming homosexual people into full membership and leadership in Christian churches is another such explosive social issue.

In his work on conflict, Alban Institute senior consultant Speed Leas defines five levels of conflict.[1] The fifth and highest level is an emotional condition in which one side wants to eliminate the other physically, destroy the opposition, kill the enemy. In the fourth level of conflict, Leas describes a lesser option, fight or flight, in which each side is willing to engage the other but both still have the freedom to withdraw from conflict. Regarding the possibility of including homosexuals in all aspects of church life, we find many people have such powerful and unexamined emotions that they enter the conversation at level four or even level five. They begin at the highest levels of enmity. We have ample ugly evidence that some homosexuals, like some doctors who perform abortions and some African Americans, have been murdered in raw, unyielding outbursts of emotional resistance. Church leaders should not underestimate the challenge of developing constructive communication when some participants feel such passion or even hate.

Emotional Grenades

Trying to talk in hateful situations can be likened to trying to worship when live grenades are rolling under the pews. Unfortunately, in the mainline congregations we know best, we have found an irrational anger that often overwhelms efforts to explore differing ideas about sexual orientation.

North American Christians are both fascinated and obsessed with spirituality and sexuality (separately and together), as is clearly seen in the preoccupations of mass media, court dockets, and best-seller lists, as well as in the agendas of denominational meetings and other national church gatherings. Protestant faith communities in particular have inherited several theological themes (outlined by Sylvia Thorson-Smith in chapter 1) that once seemed to have provided guidance for dealing with issues of sexuality and now appear to have exacerbated the tensions. In recent years, as these traditional dualisms about spirit and body, male and female, and private and public realms are challenged and redefined, congregations are struggling with the resultant theological conflicts regarding such practical questions as whether to accept homosexuals into the full life and leadership of the church.

Fear and Shame

Among the array of emotions aroused when discussing homosexuality in churches, we note especially the presence of fear and shame. Fear is rooted in the psychological and political threats brought about by revolutions in social mores that proceed with or without churches' consent. Historically both straights and gays have feared homosexuality. It has been attacked as unnatural, deviant, and disgusting, and homosexuals have felt denied, denigrated, and abused. Supporting traditional social norms, churches have declared homosexuality to be perverse, anti-Christ, satanic, and damning, branding homosexuals with the stigma and taboo that leprosy carried in Jesus' time. Yet old church standards seem increasingly out of touch with the social reality that homosexuality is recognized in the lifestyles of our neighborhoods, named in political caucuses, and casually accepted in the television programs that come into our living rooms.

In the personal experiences of many church members, however, someone who is discovered to be homosexual has been treated as a family secret to be kept hidden at all costs in the "closet." We respond to homosexuality with a shame we fear and a fear we find shameful. ("We" is inclusive because social research has shown that most people place their sexual orientation on a kind of continuum between hetero- and homosexuality, and that few people are strictly speaking only homosexual or heterosexual.) Our mixed response increases the insecurity of many who fear being shamed about even a hint of homosexual attraction. Sometimes this conflict has been so internalized (at Speed Leas' fifth level of conflict, not in society but within the psyche) that individuals turn the perception of social stigma into self-hate, and commit acts of self-inflicted murder, that is, suicide driven by shame and fear.

Our argument is this: Leaders cannot expect church members, with unexamined sexual identities and unrecognized passions, to address their differences over homosexuality as if they are dealing with less explosive matters of opinion, information, education, and negotiation. Congregations cannot broach issues that bear the emotional intensity of a nuclear reaction as if these issues pack the power of a dinner candle, as if they can be discussed following the rules of rational policy discussions and decision-making processes. When it comes to considering homosexuality, until church members first come to terms with their guts, they will not be able to use their heads.

The Reasonable Approach

Congregations that risk discussion about homosexuality have often turned to time-tested governance procedures. As is their practice, they assess the facts, examine scriptural and historical precedents, consider alternatives, encourage participation in open debate, allocate responsibilities to proper authorities, and finally reach a decision. Such churches will frequently speak of such activities as organizing forums, searching for the truth, finding scientific research data, clearly defining the issues, and studying to determine exactly what the Scripture says. When they attempt to use deeply ingrained and usually effective discussion and negotiation techniques, however, church leaders are often dismayed to find these approaches ineffective and even explosive in conflicts over homosexuality.

Traditional approaches using problem-solving procedures can help once the emotionally explosive aspects of the situation have been addressed, but not before. The unusually explosive issues of homosexuality require a significantly different approach for achieving constructive communication before seeking rational exchanges and decisions. At the earliest stages, until the emotions have been engaged in a pastoral way, facts, research, open forums, and especially debates are likely to escalate confrontations, polarize power struggles, and spark ugly exchanges that leave deep wounds in the hearts of both individuals and groups. Such organizational procedures can even permanently divide a church.

In more cautious churches, sometimes a form of contracting has been developed to contain the anticipated emotional responses. In this approach, leaders attempt to have all parties agree on a plan for the entire process of rational debate leading to a decision, allocating time for preparation, public discussion, and the congregation's or church board's adoption of a policy "when all facts are known and all the members have been heard." In our experience, this contractual plan prolongs the exchange but rarely resolves the underlying emotions involved in these explosive issues. In practice, this effort to keep the lid on irrational and unexpressed feelings may yield an increasing sense of unreality during the process and of painful betrayal at the end. Losers often still believe the process was unfair and the leaders biased—and divide the church anyway, despite their prior agreements to seek unity across disagreements. Their explosive emotional commitments guide their perceptions of "truth," and their explosive emotional energies overwhelm their early commitment "to live by the rules."

We frequently see the strong pastor as the focus of another pattern of dealing with this theological and social hot issue. Strong pastors seek to spare the church the pain of making difficult decisions or think they know better than the congregation what the answer should be. Without consultation, they decide on a course of action. Although we honor the prophetic role of religious leaders (see below), rarely have we seen the self-appointed prophet, who acts without involving congregational leaders in the decision, able to provide a lasting solution for this issue. Usually such autonomous actions deny members the chance to grow spiritually and socially, and frequently the actions of a strong pastor oppress an unseen minority within the membership.

We have also seen pastors trigger the issue by acts of natural if naive courage in the stands they take on accepting homosexual lifestyles in the community. When such symbolic actions take the congregation by surprise, members can be confused and feel betrayed by their pastor. Such independent gestures have polarized churches, inflamed irrational and unconstructive conflict, and resulted in membership loss and pastor relocation. Because the pastor's action has already occurred, it is too late for negotiation or compromise, and the opportunity for the members to restore trust and reexamine emotional foundations is problematic— though not impossible.

On one level we applaud the honest efforts of congregations to confront openly the issue of homosexuality and to plan for dealing with it. We also accept the need, under some conditions, for pastors to be strong church leaders and to be prophetic in their witness to the community. But we challenge the application of organizationally correct, by-the-book procedures to handle the explosive emotions surrounding the acceptance of homosexuals into and for the church. Congregations must be involved, but feelings that have roots in human identity are rarely resolved by facts only or by public debate. Unless members are offered ways to deal with their emotions, they will cling to old views and can as easily find fault with the procedures, people, and resulting policies as with the originating ideas themselves. They must feel that their emotions have been engaged, their fears have been honored, and their social and personal shame transformed if they are to reach a fundamental unity in Christ and in shared ministry.

Three Ways to Dismantle the Grenades

We face apparent contradictions: We believe typical, democratic decision-making procedures are inadequate as a foundation for handling
such emotionally charged material, yet the congregation must be involved. We believe that leaders must act in prophetic ways yet not break
the basic trust that binds people and pastor together in pastoral relationships. In light of these contrasting affirmations, we suggest three ways
leaders can help congregations begin to disarm emotional grenades that
threaten to explode over discussions of homosexuality. First, leaders engage the congregation in focusing more on living their faith than on dog-
matic beliefs or abstract arguments. Second, leaders encourage interpersonal communication and bonding that create shelters for safe talk about
previously unmentionable forms of love and friendship. Third, pastors
focus more on being trusted people than on being official authorities
guarding the congregation's rules or beliefs.

Share Experiences of God's Presence

At the most basic level, members of the congregation must recognize
that our identities as people of faith, both personal and congregational,
are grounded in the God whom we know and by whom we are known
in Jesus Christ. Neither individuals nor congregations can overcome
shamed identities by reasoning, arguing, doing good works, or undergo-
ing psychotherapy. We overcome shame by discovering that we are fully
known and loved the way we are. God is the ground of shameless being
for all people. Shame, that terrible secret sense of being inherently
defective, is healed by God's grace, not by arguments and not even by
therapy. The answer to shame lies not in a belief in but in a relationship
with God.

Congregations can talk about the "unspeakable" when members
remember to claim for themselves and for others the everflowing spring
of God's forgiving grace.

Discussing sexuality in the church is like building inroads through
a field of hidden explosives. In such minefields, Christians must "lift
high the cross" as both a biblical and experiential resource that gives us
the courage to risk opening the doors of everyone's closeted fears and

shames. In communal shelter we experience the awareness that each of us is above all a child of God and that all believers are collectively embraced in the body of Christ. In this awareness of God's presence, members begin to defuse the emotions—the fear and shame of our own previously hidden journeys—that have held congregations hostage to silence and sometimes to violence.

We see this sense of God's presence in the churches that share their witness in this book. Note how different doctrines, practices, and activities can be transformed into safe space in which believers share the presence of the creator/redeemer God. In these conversations, congregations reach new plateaus of "agreeing to disagree" on particularly difficult issues when they have named their mutual need for an even more universal sense of God's forgiving grace. When all recognize that each of us is sustained by grace, then everyone can express a view and know that when the dust settles, all still have a place in the love of God and God's church.

In the case studies in this book, readers will see the way these churches develop their own faith foundations to shelter their constructive conversations about the otherwise "unspeakable." Sometimes they begin with a focus on denominational standards such as biblical inerrancy or practices such as Quaker dialogue or beliefs such as the priesthood of all believers. Sometimes these discussions examine theological meanings embedded in Scripture or the practical limits of unity in diversity. Others explore tensions, such as the essential distinctions between intellectual and emotional insights into Scripture, between social justice and personal bias, between gut reactions and mature reflections.

Throughout these cases we note the shift of emphasis from static theological dogma toward the dynamic, sustaining presence of the creator God who makes all of us good, and the redeemer God who names all of us as offspring, even while we may feel fearful, uncomfortable, guilty, ashamed, or disgusted at speaking the word *homosexual*. The Christian way through fear of ourselves, fear of our differing sexual orientations, and fear of our emotionally inflamed faith family lies in experiencing God's perfect love.

Faith is our framework for addressing homosexuality, not our weapon. Faith is the common ground for our meeting, not for our arguing, winning, or voting. Until we meet and remeet on this common ground, we cannot proceed together anywhere.

Encourage Deepening Interpersonal Relationships

Just as we begin with faith as a relationship through the grace of God, so the second approach to explosive issues depends on significant, sustaining interpersonal relationships, more than on facts, rules, or democratic process. Based on these relationships, we can begin to explore our emotional fuses—the things that make us explode—in the darkness of our own and others' human sexuality. As we know God and know ourselves to be among the friends of God, we are able to relate to others as brothers and sisters in Christ, even when we fiercely disagree.

Although we recognize that congregations eventually need to utilize a democratic procedure to make their decisions, we believe these later steps should be based on a shared dynamic faith and extensive interpersonal relationships. Because a discussion of homosexuality in the church carries such heavy emotional baggage, we propose that the primary approach to the transformation of explosive feelings is more relational than rational, more like therapy than democracy. By beginning with an emphasis on interpersonal relationships, we encourage dialogue rather than debate. This kind of communication focuses on telling personal stories rather than on arguing over personal positions. Participants witness to one another through "I statements" rather than correcting one another through "you statements." Relating does not make us agree, but it usually makes us agreeable. Relating does not give us information, but it builds mutual respect. Relating does not solve problems, but it places us side by side in problem solving.

Virtually every case study in this book shows the power of developing personal relationships with known members of the congregation who are willing to "come out" and share their experiences. The effectiveness of this experience is directly related to the extent of their prior relationship and to the kind of material the people share. Some participants courageously confided that they were themselves gay or lesbian, and others that they were parent or brother or sister of a gay or lesbian person. These conversations are not theological in the usual sense. Rather, they are about the love of friends and the beauty of the earth but also about their struggle to live ordinary lives daily confronted by injustice, fear, and open abuse. In the process, old views are exposed and transformed.

Typically these conversations occur in small groups of many sorts,

where participants can share more fully. In one case the leaders of these
small groups were called "therapists," because throughout the congregation, the groups unmasked a depth of feeling, especially about the
images and experiences that made members uncomfortable with each
other and themselves. Sharing these sometimes shattering experiences
transforms relationships that nurture direct and straightforward conversation between gay and straight people who already knew each other, but
not fully. As one speaker explains, "You always seemed to love me and
accept me when I was a youth in this congregation. As it turns out, there
is a part of me that neither of us knew about then: I am a lesbian. Now
that you know more about who I am, are you still able to love and accept
me?"

Relationships make possible the "conversions" that occur when gay
and lesbian members finally feel emotionally safe to share themselves.
Whether other members end up affirming or resisting the acceptance of
homosexuals in the congregation's work, they learn to respect and affirm
previously closeted members with whom they may disagree. In this kind
of relationship, people strengthen each other by sharing their differences
and together are sustained by the continuing presence of God in Christ.

When congregational members hang with each other, their attitudes
change even when their opinions do not. They move from being dead set
against each other in contests of righteousness, information, or rhetoric
toward struggling side by side to find some way they can reach common
ground in solutions that incorporate their differences. This shift is what
Quakers have called the shift from "standing against" to "standing aside."
In relationships, members fight less among themselves and struggle more
in search of common ground and shared purposes to make the most of
their differences.

Develop Trusted Leadership

Just as "truth is the first casualty of war," so trust is often the first and
most serious casualty of extraordinarily emotional congregational conflicts. The third dimension of dismantling such emotional grenades is a
commitment to build and sustain the highest possible level of trust, particularly in congregational leadership.

In these explosive situations, pastors and lay leaders are expected to perform many functions to make the best of a difficult situation. We have already noted the foundational shelter provided by sharing the presence of God and the new vitality that comes from developing stronger interpersonal relations. Here we focus especially on the contributions of leaders.

In the cases in this book, as in our experiences with congregations, leaders have contributed in a wide variety of ways by gathering facts and building community, remembering past traditions and stories, developing biblical and theological resources, and analyzing problems and envisioning possible solutions. Although each of these is important when appropriate, we note that pastors can be serious barriers to resolving issues, and leaders can be psychologically damaged for life by these traumatic encounters.

We are especially aware of two, opposite approaches that frequently damage congregations and injure the spiritual growth of members. At one extreme are the leaders who avoid the issue when it arises. Seeking to maintain the status quo or to protect peace at any cost, they sweep the challenge to address homosexuality under the institutional rug and leave the bomb ticking to explode at a later moment of unreadiness. At the opposite extreme are pastors and church officers who feel compelled to convince others that God expects the church immediately and wholeheartedly to embrace homosexual members. When these views are experienced as prophetic injunctions or divine demands, members are denied the opportunity to work through their own feelings and hear the voice of God together.

Rather, authentic leaders must make their witness—but as testimony to their own conscience and story. Being prophetic is being personally accountable, not personally infallible. Often congregations appreciate the discomforting trigger of a prophetic witness by a leader who feels compelled to take a stand; never do congregations need the violation of a "prophetic witness" who seeks to compel them to obey, agree, or submit to that witness.

When prophetic leaders make their witness by telling their own story and exposing their own feelings, they are sharing with the congregation in the same vulnerability they ask of others when developing interpersonal relations, suggested in the second approach above. Pastors should respectfully and clearly express their own thoughts and feelings which will guide a congregation toward claiming its shared life first before determining its position on any issues. Such leaders can trust the Spirit they find prompting them to take stands to be the Spirit who also enlivens and informs the congregation they seek to lead.

Congregations embroiled with issues of homosexuality, as shown in the variety of cases throughout this book, respond well to prophetic leaders who tell their own stories with candor and invite and model dialogue with members as partners in ministry. Authentic leaders are powerfully prophetic not from heights of revelation but as peers and partners with their members, who together seek God's guidance.

Trust, which takes time to build, is the key element of leadership that sustains a congregation even amid the most explosive issues. Beyond all the different theological convictions and leadership styles, trusted pastors and church leaders bring congregations through the decision making, and they are stronger on the other side. In the crunch, members want spiritual depth, personal vulnerability, and lifelong authenticity. Pastors who live like they talk do not surprise their members when new issues arise. Personal authenticity gives prophetic professions their power. Members may not agree, but they are not surprised. Rather, they expect prophetic challenge from such a leader.

Trust can be expanded by longevity, but it is not the years that count. Rather, a pastor gains credibility from the variety of shared, intimate, transitional experiences. New pastors risk being known only by a single issue, without the accumulated capital gained by shared experiences of birth and death, sickness and health. Seasoned pastors are seen not as officeholders but through personal relationships that members can trust even when they disagree.

Conclusion

These three approaches to dismantling the emotional grenades that accompany issues of homosexuality in congregational life are not to be understood in linear or sequential fashion. They are interacting ways of approaching inflamed congregations. They occur when vulnerable, courageous leaders sustain interpersonal relationships by helping members to name the connections between faith meanings and personal journeys.

These approaches are not alone adequate for dismantling the emotional grenades embedded in issues of homosexuality. As Peter Senge has emphasized, after engaging in dialogue, organizations need to discuss what they have learned in the experience.[2] The rational processes of problem solving, debating, and decision making need to be pursued but only after a congregation has healed from inflamed distortions of identity.

We have proposed an emotional disarmament to prepare the way so that democratic rationality can best be employed. Without this foundation, congregations' standard procedures for debating and deciding differences may well wound or even destroy them. But when congregations first engage the fear and shame that inflames them, they begin problem solving in an emotional climate of divine presence and personal vulnerability. This can deepen their unity and reinforce their claims of community as they struggle through the discomforts, disagreements, and stresses in resolving issues of homosexuality.

Members who enter the conversation at the fifth level of conflict can emotionally disarm in the peace of Christ, descending to levels three, two, and one, where they can actually grow as they together make difficult choices personally and for the congregation. Sometimes, however imperfectly, they feel they are acting and living in the likeness of Christ "who, though he was in the form of God, did not regard equality with God as something to be exploited, but emptied himself, taking the form of a slave" (Phil. 2:6-7). In this spirit, the congregational space that is openly shared by all—members holding various opinions—can become both safe and redemptive.

CHAPTER 4

Rules for Talking about a Difficult Issue

Marc Kolden

At least two things ought to be established if congregational discussion about homosexuality is to have a chance of being constructive: absolute fairness and no threat of any kind hanging over the discussion. Fairness can be maintained with a combination of impartial leadership and a process known and accepted in advance by the participants. By a threat hanging over the discussion, I refer especially to a need to vote on some matter following the discussion, whether that is to exclude practicing homosexual people from the congregation or to become a congregation that explicitly welcomes such people into membership. Threats might also include some members saying they will leave if certain conclusions are reached, as well as matters related to the pastor's role or tenure.

The point is that homosexuality is such a controversial issue in many communities that without proper safeguards, it will not be possible to have a constructive and instructive conversation among people of differing opinions. If the pastor or some other leader is pushing the congregation very hard in one direction or the congregation is already deeply divided on this topic, achieving fairness may require the use of an outside facilitator or (better, in my opinion) the help of a very respected lay member already well known for impartiality who also possesses good leadership ability and people skills. My conviction is that fair discussion is almost always helpful, even if no agreement is reached, because people learn more about the matter in question and they also learn to know and understand the other people in the discussion better.

The reason for a discussion without the threat or urgency of a conseqent decision at the end of the discussion is that the need for a decisive outcome on an issue sure to be of continuing controversy puts too much pressure on the discussion. Real and honest learning will be prevented or short-circuited in order to try to control the outcome. As the old saying puts it, "It is better and more important to debate an issue without settling it than to settle an issue without debating it."

People, especially Christians, should be able to live with disagreement. Since the earliest biblical times, people believing in the same God have nevertheless found themselves led to different conclusions about what such belief means for life—not only in areas of sex but in regard to the use of money, forms of government, roles for men and women, ways of worship, and so forth. This is not to say that one opinion is as good as another or that truth is totally relative, but it is to realize that human beings think through the implications of their beliefs in different ways. Conversation about moral issues is one route to better ways of thinking. We learn from conversation partners but especially from insights larger traditions of moral reflection can bring to the discussion. Insisting that by a certain time everyone must agree or that a deciding vote must be taken violates the complexity of moral deliberation.

Christian congregations are one in faith but will differ in many other ways—not only by race, class, age, gender, and so forth, but even in their interpretations of divine laws such as "Thou shalt not kill," for example. Of course, that commandment prohibits murder, but does it apply also to abortion, capital punishment, eating meat, or fighting in war? People of good will may come to different conclusions on such matters without forfeiting their oneness in Christ. Such differing does not mean that nothing matters but that human intellect is finite and fallible when it comes to understanding God's will in certain specific cases. That is why the Bible insists that we are not saved by our works (even our good works of thinking about morality) but by faith in Christ. Our good works are important (especially for other people), but they are not ultimate. Christ's death for our sins is ultimate and it frees us to seek to know and to do God's will in our daily lives and in our congregational life.

Rules for Talking about Homosexuality

Some years ago an important Christian ethicist, Richard A. McCormick, S.J., published an article, "Rules for the Abortion Debate."[1] I have found his rules very helpful not only for groups discussing abortion but, with necessary changes, for discussing other topics as well. In the next few

pages I will follow McCormick's basic proposals and reformulate them
to apply to discussing homosexuality. My recommendation is that any
congregational group would profit by beginning a discussion on homosexuality with a full discussion of these rules. They are intended to
be formal, not substantive, so that people who disagree on substance can
still agree to converse by these rules without conceding anything.

1. Attempt to identify areas of agreement.

Doing this will help people who differ to keep from digging in too quickly to defend their positions. This is important because homosexuality is
an issue in which many people have high personal stakes.

Most people and surely most Christians on both sides of this debate
probably will agree that fidelity is good and promiscuity is bad—for
both heterosexual and homosexual people. Most also will agree that any
sort of sexual activity involving the exploitation of people is wrong. It is
important to identify this common ground.

Many Christians who think homosexual activity is wrong may nevertheless favor equal justice in civil law for homosexual people and relationships. Most Christians also will be against so-called gay bashing as
well as other forms of discrimination. Depending on the group, it may be
more difficult to achieve consensus on all of these matters, but discovering shared values can be very helpful.

Simply finding areas of agreement will not solve major differences,
but it may increase mutual respect and improve the tone of the discussion. If all the people involved are members of the same congregation,
learning to discuss controversial issues about which differences are already apparent is important for the ongoing life of the congregation in
any case.

2. Avoid the use of slogans and name-calling.

Avoid calling gay and lesbian people "perverts" or "queers." Avoid calling people who think homosexual activity is morally wrong "homopho-
bic" or "bigots." Such terms dehumanize those with whom we disagree
and make the conversational process almost impossible.

It is often the case that sincere Christians on both sides are not motivated primarily by prejudice or emotions but have carefully thought-out reasons for why they think as they do. The use of slogans and name-calling prevents people from hearing and understanding these reasons.

3. Represent opposing positions accurately and fairly.

This requires careful listening and may take some study as well. Although a heterosexual may find it difficult to understand a person who claims to have a homosexual orientation or may even find the thought of homosexual acts repulsive, that heterosexual loses nothing by learning how gay and lesbian people (or heterosexual people who support them) understand themselves and how they relate their experience to the Bible and the Christian faith. It may be difficult as well for homosexual people to understand the commitment to so-called traditional Christian sexual morality if they have experienced the claims of such a moral stance primarily in legalistic and judgmental ways.

Even if neither side is convinced by the other's arguments, fairly representing each other's positions is a way of loving one's neighbor and maintaining a constructive setting for discussion.

4. Distinguish the actor from the act.

Distinguish the person holding a position from the position itself. A person who desires to do what is good and right may nevertheless hold a faulty position or commit an immoral act. We do not have to condemn that person as a person in order to disagree with his or her position or condemn his or her action. Although some heterosexual people may be bigoted and full of hatred toward homosexuals, other heterosexuals may love their homosexual neighbor while still considering homosexual actions to be immoral on biblical or other grounds.

Homosexual people may and do make different judgments concerning the moral goodness of acting on the basis of their orientation. For example, some Roman Catholics say that same-sex inclinations are an indication that God is calling that person to celibacy. In any case, we could say that the debate is about actions, not people.

5. Try to identify the core or central issues at stake.

Many different issues and factors are mentioned in this debate, for example, the authority of the Bible, the sanctity of traditional marriage, justice for all people, the right of people to sexual fulfillment, the Creator's intention for men and women. Which issues are most important? Are some largely beside the point? How shall we decide?

Christians discussing the morality of homosexual behavior may find themselves in some tension with secular and political rhetoric, using criteria and making distinctions that nonbelievers might not recognize (for example, love for the neighbor, repentance, forgiveness). For some people, it may come down to debating the possibility of Christians accepting lifelong, monogamous, committed same-sex relationships as morally good but all other same-sex activity as morally bad—by way of analogy with traditional conservative heterosexual morality. For others, such a position would violate biblical authority or canons of justice or the insights of psychology—revealing different core issues at stake.

Seeking to identify core issues or values has the positive result of helping people to understand each other's views more deeply and increases the seriousness of the discussion. Even if people still disagree, agreeing to disagree after coming to fuller understanding will not inevitably end the discussion.

6. Admit weaknesses in one's own position.

Why? And how does this help discussion? (It is certainly not usually considered to be good political strategy!) Here people on both sides become more reflective and self-critical about their own positions. This promotes honesty and an appropriate humility that may allow people to learn things they were not open to learning previously. After all, if the issues were crystal clear and self-evident, there would not be a debate in the first place.

For example, those holding a traditional or conservative view may need to admit that some biblical passages often cited in support of this view really are about some other issue (such as ritual prostitution). Or those who simply dismiss all the biblical passages as being irrelevant to the insights of modern scientific thought about homosexuality might be more convincing if they could admit that Romans 1 is a more difficult passage to reject or reinterpret than most of the Old Testament verses.

7. Distinguish moral substance from particular formulations of moral rules and principles.

Particular formulations of moral norms will always be limited by language and human ability. Some formulations may even betray the moral substance. For example, to say that heterosexual relations are obviously the only sort permissible for human creatures because God has created us male and female may serve to reduce humanness mainly to biology and fail to enunciate a more profound or complete view of human community as God would have it exist. Or to argue that because sexual orientation is a "given," therefore homosexual activity for those who are so oriented is morally good because it is "natural" may betray Christian understandings of the relation of nature and sin; it may also ignore questions of God's will for sexual relations.

8. Distinguish morality from public policy.

It is too simple to say that if something is legal it is morally right, or that if something is morally wrong it ought to be made illegal. Although there is a close relationship between morality and civil law, they are not the same. If they are not distinguished, it will be very difficult to speak of moral convictions because conversation will tend to slide over into arguments about laws and public policy. Yet, obviously, the same moral convictions could find expression in a variety of legal and political systems. Also, because legal systems always involve sanctions for breaking laws, failing to distinguish law from morality will tend to thwart honest moral debate for fear of possible punishment for moral judgments or failings. The debate over legalizing homosexual "marriage" often overlooks this distinction by treating moral and legal aspects together without acknowledging their difference.

9. Distinguish morality from pastoral care.

Moral statements are general and seek to be universal in their application. Pastoral care focuses more particularly on the people and their context and often must deal primarily with what is possible in a given case. Even though one may be convinced that homosexual actions are morally wrong, that will not exempt one from contact with homosexual people who are sexually active, for example. In such cases, there is generally a significant difference between relating in humane or loving ways and enunciating moral norms. Being pastoral or compassionate need not mean abandoning one's moral position, just as holding to a moral position with great insistence does not need to prevent a person from acting pastorally. It may be helpful in any congregational discussion to point out that the group is probably not well suited to dealing with certain personal revelations as it attempts to discuss moral arguments. It may be necessary to address individual pastoral needs elsewhere.

10. Include the perspectives of all concerned.

Take into account the perspectives of all sides of this debate, especially those of people whose voices are not always heard in the particular congregation or group. This rule has been implicit in most of what has been said in this chapter, but it needs to be made explicit. Although in some contexts, there may be no openly gay or lesbian people present to offer their perspective, it is not difficult for others to make a case, because information is widely available and many straight people are supportive of it. In fact, one important way of increasing moral sensitivity is to learn to state positions with which one disagrees.

Some Christians who hold the traditional view opposing homosexual activity might reject this rule by arguing that it already tilts the discussion against traditional morality by allowing opposition to it equal time and presence. I think to omit gay-lesbian perspectives is sticking one's head in the sand, however, because the perspectives are so widely known and vociferously commended. It is better to look at all the positions directly than to seek to control the conversation. If the process is fair and honest, there is little to fear by allowing many perspectives to be represented. This would apply also to inclusion of conservative speakers who hold that homosexuality is not an unalterable condition. So-called political correctness should not keep a group from looking at views honestly held by people of good will. In a Christian congregational discussion, we should include the perspectives of all Christians concerned about this topic. The shared faith perspective should be enough to ensure that fair discussion will be possible.

Additional Ideas about Discussing Homosexuality

There is a lot of helpful information available about moral deliberation (discussion of moral issues).[2] It should not be ignored by moving too quickly to the debate itself. For example, there are several different models for making a case that Christians and others have used for centuries. A chart or an overview of these is helpful in allowing people to examine and understand various claims. This would include at least the following:

1. The "utilitarian" or "teleological" model, which asks about outcomes or consequences, judging an action *good* if it produces a good outcome (or the outcome is not harmful).

2. The "deontological" or "obligation" model, which asks not about outcomes but about doing one's duty or doing what is *right* or lawful.

3. The "contextual" or "responsibility" model, which asks not primarily about outcomes or doing what is lawful but rather is concerned about what is *appropriate* in a particular context. This approach emphasizes acting responsibly in the midst of complex situations and competing values.

4. A quite different approach is often called the "character" or "virtue" model, which is less concerned with acts than with the actor. The assumption here is that the person who is virtuous or who has good character will do what is morally good and right.

A moment's reflection will reveal that each of these models would use the Bible, for example, in somewhat different ways or would draw on very different portions of it, such as ideals, laws, examples, relation-ships, threats, promises, and so forth. So too, the various models might use other sources of authority and information quite differently. It is helpful to be aware that moral deliberation is itself a complicated and much debated activity.

In addition to becoming familiar with general and specific informa-tion about morality and sexual morality, I have found it very helpful to propose a process for discussion that has as its goal simply to look fairly at the most important arguments or cases on each side of a complicated issue such as homosexuality. For example, in congregations I have said I will not lead such a discussion unless we have at least three hours (per-haps four Sunday mornings, or three one-hour sessions) and that all the participants will promise to be present for all the sessions.

On the topic in question, I would spend the first hour going over the "Rules for the Debate," including handing out a sheet containing the rules. In the second hour, we would look briefly at the main arguments on one side of the issue, including some evaluation of which are solid arguments (and why) and which are weak arguments (and why). In the final hour we would look at all the arguments favoring the other side in the same way. I would take the most familiar and widely held side first and the minority position second, both because it would be most com-fortable for the people present and because they would be better pre-pared by the time they get to the minority position (which would likely be less familiar).

Then I would declare the process a success and adjourn. It would be a success because we were able to talk together without coming to blows, and we would adjourn because that was part of the process to which we agreed before beginning the discussion. Both "sides" should be satisfied that their positions were presented fairly and effectively and that they were heard respectfully. (Obviously the leader is a key here, but the rules and the process make it easier to achieve success.)

If people want to go on to some other activities, that would involve another process with other ground rules and the formation of a new group, because not all the same people would wish to continue. A next step might involve discussion of case studies, utilizing the learning al-ready achieved but less dependent on input by the leader (although the guidance someone experienced in leading case studies is important for this to be a helpful next step).

In case studies on issues as controversial as homosexuality, I have sometimes had people role-play various positions in discussing a case— assigning roles by having various types (or even stereotypes) of stances drawn out of a hat. This takes some of the pressure off and usually injects a good bit of humor, especially when people have to play roles that obviously are far from positions they actually hold. One of the values of case studies is that they encourage most people present to participate in the discussion because it is about a "case" involving people who are not present. Case studies give a little distance and allow for people to change their minds if new data or reasons are brought forward.

Conclusion

Whatever specific model for discussion a group chooses to use, participants in a conversation about homosexuality—or any difficult issue— would do well to keep in mind the two points made at the beginning of this chapter: (1) it is essential to establish a process that provides for absolute fairness and (2) there must be no threat of any kind hanging over the discussion. Of course, keeping such goals in mind and working with a set of rules such as those outlined here do not guarantee that the process will therefore be easy. It most likely will *not* be easy, and all participants probably will be challenged to grow in any number of ways. But we can have hope that the conversation will be helpful and respectful if participants are committed to recognizing one another as people freed by the work of Christ to seek to know and to do God's will.

PART 2

Talking about Homosexuality

CHAPTER 5

First Congregational Church of Fresno

Fresno, California

Frank Baldwin

First Congregational Church of Fresno (United Church of Christ) is located in a California agribusiness community with a population of nearly 500,000 and 500 churches. The region's social and political outlook is rural and conservative. Founded in 1883, the church occupies a graceful California Mission-style facility in an older central-city neighborhood and projects an atmosphere of stability and tradition. Over the years First Congregational has had a sometimes controversial reputation as a relatively free-thinking and liberal alternative to the powerful evangelical churches that dominate the local religious scene.

The congregation today has 500 members, with an average Sunday attendance of 150 and a well-supported educational ministry involving children, youth, and adults. At the height of the baby boom, the church was much larger. Some long-time members still blame clergy social activism for the decline in membership since those decades. The congregation was undeniably polarized and lost members during the struggles over civil rights, Vietnam, and the farm labor movement. Although the current era has been one of rejuvenation and growth, the institutional memory of traumatic conflict is such that even newer members have been reluctant to risk these recent gains by inviting new controversy.

Why We Started Talking

First Congregational is a multiple-staff church with two ordained ministers. At the outset of the homosexuality study the senior pastor had been in place for ten years, the associate pastor for two years, and both felt secure in an effective team ministry. The idea that First Congregational Church might consider becoming "Open and Affirming" (ONA) was nurtured privately for several years by the ministerial leadership before it was proposed for study by the membership. ONA (each letter is pronounced) is an abbreviation used in United Church of Christ parlance to indicate both an attitude toward homosexuality and a religious or moral stance adopted by a congregational vote.

About five years before the beginning of the ONA study, the ministers of the church—two heterosexual men—found themselves responding to an increasing number of requests for pastoral care and services related in some way to homosexuality. These requests came both from within the congregation and from the wider community and included such things as funerals for people who died of AIDS, advocacy for victims of gender-based discrimination, and counseling. As the pastors ministered to these various and broadening needs, their conviction grew that the whole congregation should grapple with the complex moral and spiritual questions being encountered. This conviction grew more urgent after one of them was told by the mother of a college student, "My son has recently told me that he is gay. I am shocked and desperately afraid for him. I assume that my son will no longer be welcome in the church, and therefore I also must resign. I have failed as a parent and as a Christian, and tell you in all seriousness that I am considering suicide."

While the ministers were noticing this increasing need for pastoral care touching upon homosexual issues, there seemed to be a corresponding increase in overtures from the gay and lesbian community. The church is located at the edge of the Tower District, thought of locally as "the gay neighborhood." First Congregational is the most visible Protestant church in the vicinity. There were inquiries from community groups regarding the possibility of using rooms for gay-oriented meetings and fund-raising purposes. At worship, we noticed more gay or lesbian neighbors checking out the church.

Eventually, one of the ministers agreed to perform a union ceremony for a same-sex couple. The ceremony was held on stage in a popular dinner theater and was witnessed by several hundred enthusiastic guests. After the ceremony, the minister was approached by a number of appreciative guests who said things like, "You must be very brave to be doing this," and "Does your congregation know you're here?" Somewhat puzzled by this reaction, the minister reviewed the whole experience at the next meeting of the church council. This was done not to seek approval after the fact but to brief the church leadership as to what had actually happened. The event was presented as an example of much needed pastoral outreach to gay and lesbian residents of the church's own neighborhood, and for the first time a vision was put forward that further efforts in this direction might occur. The council members were silent for a few moments. Finally, one of them said, "It's about time!" and began to applaud. The rest of the council joined in the ovation. At that moment, it was obvious that there would be support from the church leadership to engage the congregation in a process of study and discernment about homosexuality.

Structuring Our Conversation

Because initially there were no openly gay or lesbian members of the congregation to request a study of homosexuality, a constituency had to be developed. On the basis of their pastoral work, the ministers believed that a number of families in the congregation might respond to an invitation to participate in a support group to talk about gay and lesbian concerns. In January 1994, a group was gathered that continued meeting monthly throughout the year. Included were parents, siblings, children, and friends of gay and lesbian individuals. The associate pastor served as convener and facilitator. By the summer of 1994, the group was ready to begin direct advocacy for an ONA study.

A planning dialogue ensued between the gay and lesbian support group, the ministers, and a few top lay leaders of the church to clarify issues, anticipate problems, and outline a process of study and decision. The two ministers agreed on a simple division of roles and responsibilities in relation to the various phases of the process. The associate minister would be primarily involved in guiding and facilitating the study. The senior minister would focus on providing reassurance and encouragement to the entire congregation and responding to criticism and conflict as it developed. The two ministers would join in requesting that the study be undertaken and consult regularly throughout the process. For the sake of maintaining perspective and a sense of continuity throughout the ONA process, the church would actively pursue a range of familiar and positive activities that had nothing to do with homosexuality.

In October 1994, the gay and lesbian support group wrote an open letter to the church council, calling for a 12- to 16-month period of study and discussion about homosexuality, as well as a later decision about possibly writing an Open and Affirming statement for the church. Defining a rationale for undertaking this process, the letter reviewed the congregation's pastoral involvements, pointed to the need for education and understanding about homosexuality, and cited the potential for an expanded ministry of outreach to gays and lesbians and their families. At the same time, several gay or lesbian young adults who had grown up in the church and whose families were known in the congregation wrote moving letters of support, expressing why it would be important for them that the church have an ONA process. For each of these individuals, writing this letter represented an initial "coming out" to their congregation, and as such, was a step not taken lightly. Both ministers also endorsed the proposed goals and methods of the exploration. The council authorized a study "to address some issues concerning sexuality, homosexuality, and our church" and appointed a representative Open and Affirming task force to develop and guide this process.

How We Proceeded

Almost immediately, an inadvertent minor misstep underscored just how sensitive the process was likely to be. The task force enthusiastically announced its existence and goals for the ONA study in the church newsletter using a bold, oversized, headline font, which struck some readers like a declaration of war. There was a flurry of negative reaction, which indicated that a number of church members, while taken by surprise, were already certain from the outset that the proposed study of homosexuality would be either unwelcome, unnecessary, or fatally divisive. It seemed only tactful to tone down the ONA rhetoric somewhat and to provide additional explanations and reassurances. And it was also noted that some valuable insight had been gained into the range of attitudes and opinions present within the congregation.

The study of homosexuality began with an after-church educational series during Advent 1994. The first session was a showing of the video "Maybe We Are Talking about a Different God: The Story of Janie Spahr." Spahr is a lesbian Presbyterian minister whose story documents her experience in the church. The second session was a panel discussion with visitors from the local Parents, Families and Friends of Lesbians and Gays (PFLAG) support group. The third session featured another video, "Straight From the Heart," which describes what is involved for a lesbian or gay person in coming out.

Although attendance at these first meetings was respectable, averaging 15 to 20, the last session of the series attracted more than 60 participants. This was a forum about what it means to be homosexual and provided an environment in which gays and straights could talk openly and safely. Led by three young adult members of the church who are lesbian or gay, the forum was probably the most powerful and affecting of the early educational efforts in that it allowed for direct and straightforward conversation between gay and straight people who already knew each other to some extent. Participants got to know each other even better, though. As one of the panelists said, "You always seemed to love me and accept me when I was a youth in this congregation. As it turns out, there is a part of me that neither of us knew about then: I am a lesbian. Now that you know more about who I am, are you still able to love and accept me?"

The Advent series raised many questions and concerns regarding the meaning of "Open and Affirming," the focus and scope of the study process, the composition of the task force, and the danger of "splitting the church." In January 1995, a two-page question-and-answer sheet was sent to the congregation, attempting to honor and address these concerns. Although the study at this point was encountering some resistance, it was also generating a great deal of interest and support. A number of people indicated how significant it was to them to have a church in which they could feel free to openly acknowledge and affirm their gay or lesbian children, parents, siblings, and friends.

In an effort to keep these poles of opinion in conversation, in March the task force held a "Quaker dialogue" meeting to discuss the fears and hopes associated with the ONA study. Those attending, more than 75, were divided into small conversational groups in order to share feelings and listen respectfully to one another. This meeting was again helpful in providing additional information about the needs and interests of the church during the next phase of the study. One of the recurring lines of questioning concerned the implications of the word *affirming*. "Our congregation has always welcomed everyone," this argument went, "so why can't we just continue to be 'open and welcoming' or 'tolerant and accepting'?" A closely related question often heard was "Why single out homosexuals?" To specifically address these concerns, the task force brought in an articulate lesbian UCC minister to discuss "What We Mean by Affirming."

This effort was followed in April by one of the most original components of the Fresno ONA study, a presentation by a respected doctor of psychology in the congregation who methodically reviewed current scientific theories regarding the biochemical origins of human sexuality (including homosexuality). His presentation, which was reprinted and distributed on request, provided a biomedical basis for talking about homosexuality as a genetic or hormonal *orientation*, as opposed to a moral choice of one possible "lifestyle" over others. This seemed to be an especially important educational point, because opponents of gay rights frequently characterize homosexuality simplistically as the deliberate choice of an immoral lifestyle.

Because many churches actively nurture antihomosexual sentiment in their community, basing their views on a certain reading of Scripture, the task force realized that Bible study would have to play a major role in the ONA process. In the spring and fall of 1995, the two pastors taught a series of seminars looking into the relevant texts. The first classes were called "Seeking God's Wisdom Concerning Scripture and Homosexuality," and the follow-up series was entitled "The Ethics of Jesus." The pastors offered a historical-critical view of the limited number of biblical texts that deal with homosexuality, focusing on Sodom and Gomorrah (Gen. 19:1-11), verses from the Old Testament Holiness Code (Lev. 18:22 and 20:13), and Pauline texts (1 Cor. 6:9-10; Rom. 1:18-32). The literalistic interpretation of these scriptures often used to condemn homosexuals was contrasted with the teachings and example of Jesus (John 13:34-35) as well as the insights of the apostles (Gal. 3:23-29; Acts 10:1-33; 1 John 4:16-21).

Writing an ONA Statement

Early in September, the senior minister sent a pastoral letter to the congregation, reviewing the goals and accomplishments of the homosexuality study and indicating that the task force had decided to try writing an Open and Affirming statement acceptable to the church. By the end of

October, the statement had gone through several drafts and was approved by the church council to be placed on the agenda of the annual congregational meeting in January. It was written in a broad vein, affirming and celebrating the diversity existing within the congregation and declaring the church open and welcoming to people of every religious background, sexual orientation, family composition, physical and mental ability, race, age, and gender. The statement was a serious attempt to say what most members actually want to believe about their church: that it is open to everyone and affirming of all people who desire to share a life and ministry of Christian faith. In late November, the proposed ONA statement was mailed to all members with an invitation to offer a written response or participate in one of four informal gatherings planned to receive comments, critiques, and suggestions. A number of people took advantage of these opportunities, including several who remained candidly hostile to the statement and the process that had produced it.

On the Sunday of the annual meeting the senior minister was asked to preach about the proposed statement. The lectionary offered an appropriate text from Paul: "I hear there are quarrels among you ..." (1 Cor. 1:10-18). The message asserted the refining potential of respectful conflict to focus the church on things that are truly important to God. In the congregational meeting that followed the service, the ONA discussion was passionate, respectful, thorough, and conducted in accordance with firm and fair rules of parliamentary procedure. Finally, after a long pause for prayer, the vote for the statement was 98-19 (84 percent in favor) with several abstentions.

Healing the potential breach with those who had voted no (or abstained) began immediately. All reporting and interpreting of the meeting and the ONA vote stressed the validity of differing points of view and reaffirmed the unbroken unity of the church covenant with all its members. Although three or four families had left the congregation earlier in the study, in apparent objection to talking about homosexuality, there was no mass attrition as a result of the ONA vote.

Looking Back

Throughout the ONA study, First Congregational experienced a fair
amount of conflict, threats of conflict, and anxiety about conflict. Over
time, the church discovered that it could accept and embrace conflict, so
long as it was respectful and conducted within the bonds of the covenant.
Moreover, this ongoing tension within the process helped stimulate and
sustain high levels of interest and participation.

The church benefited from having a clear rationale and a carefully
worked-out process with the flexibility to adapt to changing require-
ments and new insights. Although many of the challenges had been ac-
curately anticipated in advance, there were still several surprises. For
example, it had been assumed that older, more conservative members
of the congregation would have the most difficulty with a church discussion about homosexuality. In actuality, those who seemed to have
the hardest time with ONA were the upwardly aspiring younger couples
with children, who were vulnerable to relentless social and religious
criticism from antigay peers and neighbors.

At the outset, it was suspected that a few families in the church
would have some direct, but hidden, experience with homosexuality.
Even the pastors were surprised, however, by the large number of people
who in the course of the study and vote acknowledged—many for the
first time in public—that someone they love and care about is lesbian
or gay, and therefore heavily invested themselves in the ONA process.

Since the vote, the congregation had initiated additional outreach
and advocacy in the homosexual community. Ten covenanting services
have been held in the church for same-sex couples. One year after becoming Open and Affirming, the congregation recorded its greatest annual growth in nearly two decades. A number of gay and lesbian individuals and families have been a part of this growth and seem to be
successfully finding their way into the life and work of the church.

CHAPTER 6

Dayton Avenue Presbyterian Church

Saint Paul, Minnesota

H. David Stewart

Our Congregation

Dayton Avenue Presbyterian Church is a congregation of the Presbyterian Church (U.S.A.) with a 123-year history of ministry at the corner of Dayton and Mackubin Streets in Saint Paul, Minnesota. DAPC has seen many fluctuations in membership but has been stable at approximately 180 members over the past decade. It is an urban congregation in a midsized city of the upper Midwest. Facing many of the same challenges and opportunities of urban congregations throughout the United States, the church has found the most influential to be the nearly constant sociological, economic, and racial changes in the surrounding neighborhood during the past 50 years. Although not unconcerned about financial stability, the congregation is well supported by its members' pledges, which reflect a very high level of commitment. This depth of commitment is also reflected in the average attendance for worship, which holds at between 115 and 120 during months of September to May. The membership is diverse in any of several categories, but the most immediately evident is the racial diversity of the members. The current membership is approximately 60 percent Euro-American, with the remaining 40 percent made up of African Americans, African refugee immigrants, and a smaller number of Native American and Asian Americans.

To fully appreciate the dynamics of our discussions of homosexuality, it is important to understand the history from which this diverse identity emerges. From the time of its founding in 1874, Dayton Avenue Presbyterian Church quickly became a prosperous and well established congregation. Twelve years later, the congregation built the large red sandstone sanctuary it occupies today. A second addition was added approximately 14 years afterward. At the height of its numerical membership, in the first quarter of this century with more than 600 members, the congregation reflected the neighborhood: white, generally well educated, middle- and upper-middle-class professionals, business owners, and others who occupied respected positions within the community. Some of the first changes in the community came in the 20s and 30s, when a number of European immigrants settled in the neighborhood and though not quite as well established economically, were still welcomed into the congregation. Subsequent changes in the neighborhood, especially a rather rapid change in the racial make-up of the neighborhood following WWII, were not immediately reflected or welcomed in the congregation. The congregation did not immediately find ways or willingness to welcome these new, mostly African-American neighbors into the congregation, but when faced with demise in the late 50s and early 60s, it finally decided to open its doors to the community around it.

Today Dayton Avenue Presbyterian Church continues in ministry as a multiracial, multinational congregation, which is probably our most significant identifying mark and a significant factor in every aspect of our mission and ministry. This diversity is one of the most important factors identified by new members in their decision to join our congregation. It was clearly a very significant factor in our discussions regarding human sexuality and church leadership.

Another significant part of our congregational identity is its long history of community involvement and social justice ministry. Part of the redevelopment of the congregation was linked to a strategy of community outreach through social programming. Dayton Avenue Presbyterian Church is the sponsoring organization for Liberty Plaza, a low- to moderate-income housing project of 174 units just a block and a half from the building. The plaza is nearing its 30th anniversary and remains one of the best operated housing projects in the city of Saint Paul. Over the past 25 years, the congregation has offered its building to numerous community and governmental programs. One of the largest neighborhood Women, Infant and Children (WIC) clinics in Saint Paul has operated in the church building for nearly 20 years. We currently house programs for ECFE, the Hmong Media Council, the Ramsey County Foster Care, Mentors of Ramsey County, an AA group (of 20 years' standing), an EA group, and four NA groups.

In the past, Dayton Avenue Presbyterian Church has also housed an Eritrean culture and language school, a Montessori school, chemical abuse programs, a neighborhood justice and anticrime council, and a number of other agencies or programs. The congregation has operated a free store for clothing and household items for 20 years. All of this indicates the level of commitment to social ministry this congregation has exhibited over the past three decades. For many years, this commitment to social action and justice has been a significant criterion for members choosing to join the congregation.

Our Conversations

It was within this context of diversity and concern for social justice that the decision to explore issues of human sexuality and church leadership was made, in response to the call of our denomination for every governing body of the church to study and engage in dialogue on the issue of human sexuality and church leadership. The DAPC Social Action Committee, when it became aware that the Presbyterian Church had made the request of congregations, recommended to the session (governing board) that we engage in the study and dialogue, and was charged with designing the method of study. Their recommendation was to establish one year of exploration and conversation.

As these plans were discussed, it was interesting to note that there were a couple of small groups within the congregation who were not convinced it was necessary to spend this much time talking. One group was of the opinion that the Bible was absolutely clear on the "sinfulness" of homosexuality, so "what's to be discussed?" A second group that felt the discussions were unnecessary expressed their position in terms similar to this: "It's a matter of injustice, and we of DAPC have long supported Christian justice issues—so why spend so much time on something that is so obvious?"

Most members of the congregation, however, were uncommitted, although there seemed to be some reluctance to open discussion. This reluctance seemed to emerge from a couple of different attitudes toward conversations about the issues of sexuality in general. The first was one expressed by those members who really knew very little about homosexuality, in part because it was never talked about openly through most of their lives. A second group seemed to want to avoid the conversation because it offered the possibility of conflict and seemed to take energy away from other equally important issues, a major concern in a busy congregation that has limited resources of time and energy available for its many tasks and activities.

Weighing all these considerations, the session agreed to implement the denomination's request to engage in dialogue during the calendar year 1995. The plans for congregational dialogue called for a minimum of four all-church open forums, which were designed so members could listen to the questions, concerns, commitments, and positions of their fellow members. In addition, outside resource people were included in various activities during the course of the year. Several multiweek sessions of the adult education class were devoted to topics pertinent to human sexuality, biblical authority, the More Light movement in the Presbyterian denomination,[1] and other related topics. Several videos from various sources were used with a fair amount of effectiveness. In the regular worship services, the issue of homosexuality was addressed through prayers for our dialogue, congregational updates and invitations, and a sermon that included the personal testimony of one member whose gay son grew up in this congregation.

Every attempt was made to be as inclusive of the full spectrum of the congregation as possible. Invitations were made widely and repeatedly in the newsletter and weekly bulletins. Personal invitations by members of the social action committee and session were extended whenever possible and critical. At the midpoint of the year, the plan was adjusted when it was perceived that the discussions were not as inclusive as the planning committee desired. Every identifiable group of the church was asked to schedule discussion time during meetings in September or October, and the social action committee undertook the task of training discussion leaders from each group to lead these conversations. Given the differences of opinion that were known to exist among the members of the congregation, every gathering was prefaced with a statement that the purpose of the dialogues was to discover our understandings, to learn more about the issues of sexuality and sexual orientation, and to determine what our Christian response might be. We attempted to make it clear that although we might not agree completely about every aspect of our discussions, one of the Preliminary Principles of the Presbyterian church is that "there are truths and forms with respect to which men [sic] of good characters and principles may differ. And in all these we think it is the duty both of private Christians and societies to exercise mutual forbearance toward each other" (*Presbyterian Book of Order* G-1.0305).

Although it was very clear at the end of the year that there were still differences of opinion, I would say that we were able to complete the discussions without lasting conflict. Subsequent to these dialogues, the session adopted a statement of openness and affirmation and presented it to the congregation at the annual meeting. Some DAPC members were disappointed that the statement was adopted and do not concur with it, but there was a great outpouring of concern for those members by the supporters of the statement. One of the session members likened the discussion and the outcome to the kind of discussions that would occur within a family, in which "we may not always agree, but we are family nonetheless." Although it had been suggested that the decision to discuss issues of sexual orientation in a church would inevitably lead to the loss of members, that has not been the case for our congregation. Up to this time, we have had no members withdraw from membership as a result of the dialogue or the adoption of the statement of openness and affirmation.

The Learning Curve

A turning point in our dialogue came with the realization that the issue was not impersonal but embodied in the lives of people known to us in our congregation. That pivotal moment in our year of exploration came when a deeply respected member of our congregation, with the permission of her son, described the pain and isolation she and her family felt in regard to her son's sexual orientation. Her son is gay and African American. His mother's assessment was that the congregation had been very supportive of and helpful to him in regard to racial issues. His church was totally silent, however, when it came to his sexual orientation. This denial was all the more troubling in contrast to the support he received as an African American. This information, shared in the context of a regular worship service, allowed us to be prayerful about our failures to minister to this family and reminded us that we might be guilty of withholding true pastoral care from others within our community, specifically those who are gay or lesbian and their families, as they face systematic rejection and oppression by society, the church included.

We also learned to respect one another more deeply across the differences we have about certain specific issues. Although DAPC has long celebrated its diversity, I believe that the year of dialogue about sexual orientation forced us to recognize that there are huge challenges to living together in a diverse community. These challenges are countered by equally powerful joys and affirmations, but it takes a great deal of work and dedication to continue as a congregation that seeks to "exemplify the kingdom of God." We learned that it is very important to learn one another's stories, for it is out of these stories that our belief and value systems emerge. To live in a community of diversity requires that we learn to honor and respect the faith history that each of us brings to the community.

Several members reported to me that the dialogue allowed them to really explore their own belief systems more thoroughly than they had previously. It was no longer enough to hold an opinion about homosexuality, either pro or con, after the year of discussions required of the participants to reflect on their theology. The net result for a number of the members was a deepening appreciation for and understanding of their own faith expressions.

Finally, I believe we learned that we can tackle tough issues about which we may have substantively different opinions and theological stances, and discuss these things in ways that do not destroy the bonds of the Spirit that make us a community. If we were to engage in this sort of discussion again, I think that we might begin differently. What emerged from our discussions on homosexuality was that we needed to know and honor each others' personal, familial, and theological histories before we could really honor and respect the differences of opinion we held toward the issue of sexual orientation. Alongside our discussions regarding homosexuality, an ongoing group, the reconciliation and diversity task force, formed with the purpose of deepening our understanding of our rich individual histories in the context of the church community.

Lessons in Hindsight

When planning for these sessions, we made the assumption that most everyone would be familiar with the "traditional" church position regarding homosexuality. Given this assumption, little outside input and few resources were brought to the congregation to articulate the historical point of view. We discovered two flaws in this assumption. First, only a few people really had much understanding of the church's stand on homosexuality. In fact, many of the congregation really had very little working knowledge about homosexuality at all. The second weakness of the assumption was that those of the congregation who hold the traditional view felt as if the discussions were skewed and did not give their traditional point of view equal time.

Were we to enter into these discussions again, it would be very helpful to avoid any assumptions about people's understanding and to try to seek more balance in the presentations of biblical, medical, and sociological information. I also wonder if we spent the right amount of time in discussions. This was very hard to judge. Some said we spent far too much time in discussions, others felt we could have gone on for a much longer period, with the idea that consensus was the most important goal. Because full consensus was unlikely ever to occur, some sort of deadline was absolutely necessary. A final change I would make in our methodology would be to incorporate ways to broaden the small-group approach that was added to our original plans for discussion. In fact, a dialogue methodology that incorporated small groups from beginning to end, with plenary gatherings to hear the reports of the small groups, might expand the percentage of involvement and allow groups to delve more deeply into the subject material in an environment in which trust has been established. Finally, the biblical portions of the study could have been expanded, especially exploration of how we read the Bible and how we discover and respond to its authority for our lives.

In the end the greatest benefit to our congregation was the discovery that we are a community of faith sustained by God's presence. God has a mission in mind for us that is greater than our differences about the issue of homosexuality or any other challenging topic. In fact, our diversity, which we feel called by God to exemplify as a witness to the covenant community of the future, both challenges us with differences of opinion and allows us to discover riches in the many perspectives we bring to our community. A second benefit is that a number of members truly spent time in serious theological and biblical reflection and discovered that it can be very meaningful, enriching, and uplifting. Several members have reported a desire to continue that sort of activity in some manner in the future. The desire to continue to get to know and trust one another at deeper levels is also a very positive outcome of the study.

CHAPTER 7

Zion United Church of Christ

Henderson, Kentucky

J. Bennett Guess

The study of homosexuality became more than a set of issues to the
people of Zion United Church of Christ in Henderson, Kentucky. Instead, it became the heart of an evangelistic renewal movement that
grew to include many different types of individuals who have felt unwelcome or underappreciated in the Christian community. It became
the crux of the congregation's identity as an intentional community un-
ashamedly committed to inclusive evangelism—sharing good news to
all God's people and receiving people as they are.

Zion United Church of Christ is located in the historic downtown
area of Henderson, an industrial city of about 30,000 people along the
Ohio River in northwestern Kentucky. Organized in 1871 as a German
Evangelical Church (which would later become part of the United
Church of Christ through a series of denominational mergers), the congregation still worships in its original brick sanctuary built in 1873. For
the majority of its history, the church maintained a strong identification
with its immigrant past.

The sanctuary is intimate and ornate, and no more than 130 people
can crowd into a Sunday service. Zion sits on a busy street corner at the
edge of the central business district in one of the city's most racially and
economically diverse neighborhoods. Historic mansions and old, small,
shotgun-style mill housing commingle alongside wide city streets. The
city itself sits on the river's edge just across from Evansville, Indiana,
and the metropolitan area population is about 314,000.

Relying heavily on the neighborhood's many German families to
fill the pews, the congregation remained a small but healthy, theologically conservative church with a liberal commitment to mission and
outreach. Although far from considering itself an activist congregation,

the church and its pastor did play a major role in working for the integration of public schools in the 1950s. And for years the church sponsored a scouting troop composed almost equally of Christians and Jews. The church gave generously to cooperative ministries and worked year-round on a bazaar that benefited area charities.

By the late 1980s, however, the church was in decline. Ethnic heritage alone was not enough to retain or attract church members who were now seeking out the more inviting programs and activities of larger congregations. "The little German church" was getting smaller every Sunday. By 1992, the church officially listed 32 members, of whom only about 15 were active. Most were in their 80s and 90s. These few elderly members knew that drastic changes would have to be made in order to revive their old dying church, and they were willing to try anything.

I was a young United Methodist pastor, a recent graduate of Vanderbilt University Divinity School. While serving a small, rural parish, I was agonizing over my future as an ordained United Methodist Church pastor who was also gay. I hoped the 1992 General Conference of the UMC, which was set to hear a report from a study committee on homosexuality, would create a more welcoming atmosphere for lesbian and gay clergy. But the General Conference decided to ignore the results of its own study. It was then that I finished transferring my credentials to the United Church of Christ, hoping to find there more acceptance as a gay man.

I had long dreamed of serving within a religious community wholeheartedly committed to peace and justice ministries. I also dreamed that my hometown—Henderson, Kentucky—could one day have a church that was not afraid to welcome strangers and awaken the too-often sleeping conscience of a mostly uninvolved Christian culture. Fortunately, Zion UCC in Henderson was desperate for young pastoral leadership, and I was desperate for a place to do ministry. As it turned out, Zion became the ideal place to implement a model of Christian community based on an inclusive, just-peace covenant theology similar to those well-known intentional communities such as Koinonia Farms near Americus, Georgia; Sojourners in Chicago and Washington, D.C.; or Church of the Saviour in Washington, D.C.

Today, the Zion UCC community includes about 230 members and friends. Written annual covenants by individual members are central to the life and work of the community and its ministries. A consensus style of decision making has been adopted for the congregation and its teams and committees. The church's ministries include outreach to people with disabilities, an on-site Planned Parenthood family planning clinic for low-income neighborhood residents, visual and performing arts programs, the region's HIV/AIDS prevention and case management organization, and various nontraditional religious education programs. In 1994, the church opened the Paff Haus Peace and Justice Community Center in an adjacent historic building, which serves as the headquarters for about 15 progressive organizations.

Average worship attendance is above 100 on most Sunday mornings. A Sunday evening Quaker-style service attracts another 15 to 25 people, and a midweek Eucharist attracts an additional 10 to 20 people. Immediate plans call for an additional traditional worship service on Saturday evenings. Zion UCC is a regional church, often drawing members and visitors from a 100-mile radius. More than 2,000 people have visited Zion Church in the last four years. Many are unchurched seekers who are drawn to the church's commitment to building intentional community and celebrating diversity. The congregation is predominately white, although there are a few African-American and Hispanic members. The members' ages, educational backgrounds, employment experiences, and income levels are quite diverse. About 30 percent of the church membership is openly gay or lesbian. Many of the new members are young heterosexual couples with children, who said they wanted to attend Zion Church because they wanted their children to learn an appreciation for diversity.

Getting Ready to Study

Many people incorrectly assume that the presence of an openly gay or lesbian pastor indicates some widespread congregational commitment to lesbian and gay issues. This was not the case at Zion during my first two years, however. My sexual orientation was not hidden from the original dozen elderly members who hired me, but neither did they view it as central to my ministry or pastoral identity. The fact that I did not lie about my sexual orientation certainly provided for some good gossip in our town but not necessarily among our own members.

During my first two years at Zion, I focused on being an effective pastor, loving my parishioners, leading effective worship services, and continually stating and restating our vision of becoming a renewed and vibrant congregation. During this time, the congregation's identity as a justice and peace community was established, thanks in part to our congregation's 1993 decision to enter into a six-month just-peace church study, as requested of all UCC congregations in 1985 by our denomination's General Synod. In hindsight, this churchwide study taught us the art and technique of congregational self-study—a lesson that would later give us insight into developing a methodology for studying issues surrounding homosexuality. Finally, in late 1993, several members—including me—decided Zion should begin thinking about becoming an Open and Affirming (ONA) congregation within the UCC. The study process, many members believed, would be a complement to the just-peace resolution we had passed earlier that same year. At that time, we had about 85 members.

Several members believed a formal process was not necessary. "We already welcome gay and lesbian people," some said. Three closeted gay men, who would eventually leave the congregation, felt the church should somehow remain in the closet about its affirmation of lesbian and gay people. "I don't want my identity associated with such a gay-affirming church," they said, indicating that they loved our church's welcoming stance but did not want everyone to know about it. Most members thought that if there was an official list of gay-affirming churches, we should be on it. At the same time, almost all agreed that having our name on a list was secondary to truly embodying the ONA commitment. The worst thing we could do, many said, was to state that we were open and affirming of gay and lesbian people if, in actuality, we were not.

The Step-by-Step Process

Step 1

We initiated a preliminary study to see if a more intricate study was in order. Ten copies of an introductory ONA film were distributed throughout the congregation in order to gauge initial response to the ONA study idea. Efforts were made to ensure that everyone, including our oldest members, was included in this initial step. The response was positive. And our efforts to include everyone and to be open and direct about what we were thinking about doing was a definite plus. No one could say he or she was not consulted.

Step 2

Our administrative board called for a six-month study on homosexuality throughout our church community. A leadership team was assembled and was charged with developing a timetable for our ONA study. At this point, I distanced myself from the process, because I did not want this study to become a referendum on my pastorate or my personal identity.

From the beginning, several people insisted that any possible ONA statement should be careful to communicate the idea that our ONA journey was to be seen as only one step toward our becoming the inclusive community we believed God was calling us to be. We were careful to realize that we must continually recognize the presence of all forms of prejudice among us and repeatedly confess our unwillingness to rid ourselves of that prejudice. Even after a congregation becomes ONA, there will be cause for further study, confession, and reconciliation.

Step 3

One of the key ingredients of our success happened here. We organized a churchwide conversation one Sunday immediately following morning worship. Five well-trained therapists, all from outside our congregation, were invited to lead us in an honest discussion about the hopes and fears this ONA process would create in and among us. Our facilitators divided the 65 attendees into five groups, where individuals could share their deepest feelings about homosexuality, what they needed to know, and what our churchwide study should include. I, meanwhile, left the building altogether and went in search of 15 large pizzas, which were to be part of the reward for those attending!

About an hour later, we reassembled, ate lunch, and heard comments from our guest therapists, who relayed the information each group had presented to them. The facilitators talked about where the congregation was and what was required in order to meet the needs of our members. The congregation provided feedback on the accuracy of the therapists' findings. From this point, we had a good grasp of the issues that would need to be addressed. Specifically, the congregation said it desired more information on: (1) the practical aspects of being Open and Affirming; (2) safety concerns for our pastors, members, and property; (3) sound biblical education, including a biblical self-defense plan to counter antigay fundamentalists; (4) specific ways to make our statement genuine and concrete; (5) the stories of lesbian and gay people from within and outside the church; and (6) HIV/AIDS ministry, education, and prevention.

For the most part, the congregation wanted to proceed with the study and to structure it in a way that would meet the educational needs of the highest possible number of members. But there were comments about public displays of affection and same-sex commitment ceremonies, and blanket statements concerning the inappropriateness of certain behaviors revealed some members' discomfort. Some lamented that we certainly did not want to become a "gay church."

Step 4

We organized several work sessions for the administrative board and the congregation as a whole. These sessions included programs on inclusive language for the gay community, scriptural support for welcoming lesbian, gay, bisexual, and transgendered people, bias-related violence against the gay community, legal issues affecting gay people and same-sex couples, and scientific information regarding the development of sexual orientation. We found that facilitators from outside the congregation provided a greater sense of validity for the study process itself and allowed participants to be more honest. Our worship services included some contemporary readings from lesbian and gay authors, and community meals held after worship on the first Sunday of each month provided a speak-out time for members to share their feelings about the process in general. Members were invited to attend several gatherings where the specific wording of our ONA statement was discussed. Several members felt we were ready to vote long before we did, but just trying on and living with the idea that we would become an ONA congregation was good for us. We wanted the congregation's voting process to come only after the work had been diligently undertaken.

As the pastor, I never preached on the subject of becoming ONA. This was not a conscious decision but is an interesting fact to some who hear our story. In fact, if I assumed any role during this process, it was to equate this decision to our shared commitment to evangelism and a re-claimed sense of biblical Christianity.

Step 5

On May 22, 1994, a congregational meeting was held to vote on the proposed ONA resolution. Eighty people attended the meeting, and members now recall some degree of nervousness among us, not necessar-ily that we would not approve the measure but instead that everyone would still retain a deep sense of community after the decision. Because we had a strong commitment to consensus building, the congregation's leaders were prepared, if necessary, to postpone the vote if any new concerns were raised. But the meeting turned into a time of honest shar-ing about how deeply people loved our church. When the question was asked by the church president, "Does everyone stand within the consen-sus that we declare ourselves to be an Open and Affirming congrega-tion?" the vote was unanimous, 80-0. All of the older, long-time mem-bers were present at the meeting and voted in favor of the ONA resolu-tion.

Step 6

This step has a life of its own. It continues to this day and has definitely been the most difficult step: to embody the vision of being Open and Affirming, to receive the joys and benefits with humility, and to face the opposition to our congregation that this prophetic statement has created.

Following our all-church vote, we decided simply to publish our ONA statement in the local gay community newspaper, *The Tri-State Alliance News*. When a reporter at the *Evansville Courier*—the city's daily newspaper—noticed our advertisement, she felt it was a worthy news story. When she contacted me, my initial gut response was to hush the story, but I realized that we certainly could not silence our stated welcome. It should, in fact, be a matter of congregational pride. What followed was a front-page story, then another, and then another. Readers' letters, on both sides, filled the editorial pages of area newspapers. The Associated Press sent reporters, and the *Louisville Courier-Journal* ran a front-page story about the developing feud in Henderson. In many ways, Zion UCC became the small-town symbol of a hotly contested national church debate.

Local fundamentalist ministers joined together to condemn our congregation as not a part of "the true church of Jesus Christ." The pastor of a large Southern Baptist congregation initiated steps to ostracize our church from ecumenical church life, insisting that the area ministers' alliance, a group of interdenominational ministers, publicly condemn homosexuality. The antigay pastors insisted they would remove themselves from the alliance if either Zion UCC or I were allowed to participate in any ecumenical activities. The ministerial association refused to address the issue, however, and restated its belief that any duly ordained pastor in the county was to be a member of the association. Other ecumenical organizations, of course, balked at the idea of refusing our involvement or returning cash donations received from our congregation.

Habitat for Humanity, which had been meeting at the Paff Haus (our adjacent peace and justice center) and was provided free office space there, did decide during the controversy to relocate to other space. Since then, Habitat's board of directors and committees have traveled to various churches for meetings but have not returned to Zion UCC. Our congregation, however, the first in the city to join Habitat's Covenant Church Program, does remain supportive of Habitat's vital ministry despite some hurt feelings among our members.

Reaction from within our own denomination, the United Church of Christ, has ranged from great praise at the national and conference levels to constant criticism from a small handful of antigay UCC pastors in the Evansville/Tri-State Association of UCC churches, of which our congregation is a member. But mostly, UCC churches and pastors have respected the breadth and depth our renewed faith community adds to the UCC family of churches in our region.

Our process will probably not be a typical one. It is tempered by my presence as an openly gay pastor and by our once-dying congregation's search to find new avenues for growth and service. But still, we believe our process was undertaken with integrity and with a great deal of respect for individual participation. Some observers might conclude that the publicity and controversy that followed our decision were negatives. Yet, although we did not pursue it, the intense media attention unified our intentional community. The public nature of our study empowered us to state clearly among ourselves and for others the kind of church we intend to be and to choose between silence and justice. As in all such defining moments when bold professions are made, we found the beautiful depth of a gospel faith courageously witnessed and rightly lived.

CHAPTER 8

Trinity United Methodist Church
Atlanta, Georgia

Mark Reeve

Trinity United Methodist Church, founded in 1853, is the second oldest
UMC congregation in Atlanta. The red brick neo-Gothic sanctuary has
been a landmark among the government office buildings so long that the
street beside our education building is called Trinity Avenue. Many
other congregations in the metro area can trace their history to Trinity's
mission projects. In the 1930s, the congregation's membership reached
its peak at 1283. Now membership stands at about 250, with average
worship attendance of 100. Over the years, Trinity has counted gover-
nors and other officials among its active members. Governor John
Marshall Slaton is reputed to have prayed at the altar here before par-
doning Leo Frank, the Jewish businessman accused of murdering a young
factory girl. The soul-searching decision cost Slaton his career.

Trinity has a number of theologically trained members and is
known for its strong music program. But as the automobile and shifting
residential patterns took their toll on Trinity's membership beginning in
the 1950s, the commitment to justice and to ministries for the inner city
strengthened. Members and pastors alike became known for their leadership in civil rights—a cause no less popular in Atlanta at that time than
is support for lesbian, gay, bisexual, and transgendered rights today.

Later the congregation sponsored ministries in a nearby housing
project and among the city's other poor and oppressed people. Whereas
there had been a time when Trinity had been a source of support for any
number of smaller or struggling congregations, now wealthier congregations began adding Trinity to their mission budgets. That outside financial support remains crucial to both the operational budget and mission
budgets of the congregation to this day.

I first came to Trinity to work as the church secretary. A bisexual, at that time I had been working for an interfaith organization that promoted peace and various economic and racial justice issues. Trinity was one of our strongest supporting congregations, and I felt very comfortable working in the office there. The much beloved choir director organist was widely known to be gay, a fact that was nonetheless seldom commented upon. I joined the congregation after working at Trinity for a year.

The Beginnings of Controversy

Not long after that, the congregation was rocked with controversy. Our choir director joined the Atlanta Gay Men's Chorus. As that group grew, they needed regular practice space. All manner of peace and justice groups had met at Trinity over the years, so it was natural for the chorus to approach the pastor about holding auditions and rehearsals at Trinity. As I recall the situation, the pastor forgot to bring the issue up with the administrative council, but because he had promised the chorus an answer, he simply gave them permission to use the building. If no one batted an eyelash about the Socialist Workers Party regularly meeting here, he apparently reasoned, who would mind the Gay Men's Chorus rehearsing in the building? News slowly leaked out in the congregation that the group was meeting at Trinity.

Then a notice appeared in the Atlanta daily newspaper that the Atlanta Gay Men's Chorus was having auditions at Trinity United Methodist Church. As luck would have it, the notice appeared at the top of a right hand page, a position so noticeable that advertisers pay dearly for it. We quickly learned just how prominent a position this was. Lots of people saw the notice, and rumors spread like wildfire through North Georgia United Methodist circles. Rumors reached financial supporters, the district superintendent, and even the bishop. Some people were claiming the Gay Men's Chorus had designs on supplanting the congregation's own choir on Sunday mornings!

Emergency meetings ensued, and a Bible study was held in Sunday school. In the end, the administrative council offered to lease space to the chorus, with the rent to cover all utilities and other costs to the congregation. Supporters of the chorus tried to negotiate for a less expensive lease and for an offer that had a more inviting tone to it. But the chorus lost, and not surprisingly, the chorus declined Trinity's offer and looked for a more welcoming location to rehearse.

Still, our choir director remained on staff. The church remained loyal to him and extended that welcome to his friends. When his partner was killed in an auto accident, members of the congregation turned out in substantial numbers for the memorial service. Over the years other gay men joined and contributed greatly to the life of the congregation.

Social Ministry Efforts

Trinity's main focus in the past decade and a half has been ministries with homeless men and women. In the winter of 1982 a night shelter opened in the basement, providing sleeping pads and blankets for 30 men during the coldest months of the year. A few months later a soup kitchen was established and members began serving dinner on Sunday, when other meal programs in the city are closed. The soup kitchen quickly began serving up to 800 meals every Sunday, and the night shelter has evolved into a program to help homeless men get themselves out of the downward spiral. The congregation also supports a transitional house for homeless men. And more recently, the congregation has begun to respond to the needs of people who are HIV-positive or who have AIDS.

In addition to homelessness, over much of that period work for peace in Central America and against racism in this country had the attention of our social concerns committee. About the time Washington Square in New York City and Grant Park-Aldersgate here in Atlanta came to be among the earliest Reconciling congregations, I was part of a network opposing the Trident submarine base at Kings Bay Georgia and the White Train that carried nuclear warheads by rail through our state. I was well supported by the congregation, even when I spent almost two months at a county correctional institution for civil disobedience opposing the train.

Variations of my story applied to the other gay members of the congregation as well. In general, we were very involved in issues supported by the social concerns committee. Still, the "homosexual issue" was obviously painful to many people. But the unspoken consensus seemed to be that members of the congregation supported one another in many wonderful ways, so why raise waves by introducing this potentially difficult issue? Better to put the energy into cultural events or political action on issues more amenable to all.

The Houston Declaration

A comfortable Southern variation of "don't ask, don't tell" could have prevailed for a long time but for the rising power of the religious right. In 1992 a group of United Methodist clergy adopted the "Houston Declaration," attempting to influence the General Conference to move in more conservative directions on the issue of homosexuality. In April 1995, many of the same conservative leaders formed the "Confessing Movement" and issued a "confessional statement." The statement argues that "condoning homosexual practice" and "ignoring the Church's long-standing protection of the unborn and the mother" are abhorrent to God. Many Trinity members were alarmed by what seemed to be the movement's intention "to impose a narrowly defined orthodoxy" on the denomination, and members of Trinity who were well versed in both United Methodist politics and theology issued a rebuttal.

When the Confessing Movement announced it would convene in Atlanta in April 1995 for its second national meeting, the need to respond became a major priority for the congregation. We agreed whole-heartedly with the movement's emphasis on the centrality of Jesus Christ. But the Confessing Movement document challenged "the diversity and inclusiveness that have marked Methodism since its beginnings as an eighteenth-century reform movement."[1]

E-mail flew during the spring of 1995 as members drafted a response to the Confessing Movement before the Atlanta meeting. Several preliminary drafts were presented to the congregation, and the text was discussed thoroughly. The final product was titled "A Call for Renewal of Theology and Mission in the United Methodist Church." It reads in part:

> The most important mission of the church is to proclaim the Good News of Jesus Christ announcing that God sets people free from all forms of evil and equips them for a life of holiness. John Wesley's understanding of holiness includes creating a more just social order for everyone, especially the poor, widows and orphans, slaves, and

the sick. Faithfulness to this heritage demands that we continue to work toward a social order in which people of various races and ethnicities, both genders, all social and economic classes, and different sexual orientations can live together lovingly and justly.

To supporters of this response, this means we must focus "on the forces in today's world that diminish life for everyone, especially those who are poor and otherwise pushed to the margins of life."[2] The Call for Renewal also invited the Confessing Movement to join us "in opposing the persecution of any person simply because of their religion, race, ethnic background, gender, sexual orientation, economic station, physical or mental condition, and in opposing all other forms of oppression, as sins against God and Jesus Christ."[3] In the end, the Call for Renewal was endorsed by Methodists across the country and received widespread attention in the United Methodist press.

A Reconciling Congregation

In the summer of 1996, I attended the Reconciling Congregation (RC) Convocation in Saint Paul, Minnesota. Not surprisingly, widespread support was expressed for Trinity's Call for Renewal. Many in the RC movement pointed out that the paragraphs quoted above constituted a Reconciling Congregation statement, if we wanted to claim that description.

I came back from the convocation and wrote in a report to the congregation:

Indeed, it seems to me that becoming a Reconciling Congregation is not about joining another cause, nor taking on yet another ministry. The fact is, Trinity is already a welcoming congregation ... and has been for years. Trinity has had many gay, lesbian, and bisexual members and friends over the years, and we have participated fully in the life of the congregation. I would go so far as to say that joining the RC program isn't really a social justice issue at all—though, of course, human rights and civil liberties for all people continue to be important justice issues. At its heart, I believe the RC program is about Evangelism and Pastoral Care. I want others in the metro-Atlanta area who feel alienated from God's loving Grace to know that they have available a church home at Trinity United Methodist Church.

Others in the congregation concurred that we really should come out explicitly as a Reconciling Congregation. A proposal was brought from the outreach committee to the administrative council, and a task force, of which I became a member, was formed to provide leadership for a congregation-wide study of the issue. Two adult Sunday school classes used a resource called "The Church Studies Homosexuality."[4]

Knowing how much pain the issue had caused in years past, the task force emphasized the positive parts of the congregation's involvement with the issue. A pamphlet issued by the task force presenting the case before the congregation stated: "By the Guidelines of the Reconciling Congregation program of the United Methodist Church, we have already met the expectations of becoming a Reconciling Congregation. All of them, except one. For years Trinity has considered itself a Reconciling Congregation without officially registering as one."

We recognized that making a statement of openness meant we might receive new members who would affect the life of the congregation, as new members inevitably do in any healthy community. But we assured the congregation that declaring ourselves to be reconciling in no way meant we would suddenly devote major resources to sexuality issues.

The task force and our pastor were all determined that we wanted as close to consensus as we could get. We wanted to make a statement about including people. Although everyone might not agree with our position on homosexuality, it would certainly be counter to that principle if the statement itself made anyone feel excluded.

Shortly before the church conference in December 1995, we realized we did not have consensus and did not take a vote. Instead, we agreed to call a church conference in the spring of 1996. Further study and discussion followed. The church conference itself, which addressed only this issue, was relaxed and friendly. The reconciling statement was adopted with few abstentions or no votes. As far as we know, we might have lost one family as a result of adopting the statement.

Now the challenge to the congregation is to make this statement meaningful. It is still clear that sexual identity issues are not going to become a major part of Trinity's ministry. But small changes are evident.

The bulletin on Sunday always carries a notice that we are a Reconciling Congregation and that all are welcome. Notices have been placed in local gay community newspapers and on the Internet. More recently, the congregation has made a decided effort to claim its status as a Reconciling Congregation. For example, during the summer Olympics held in Atlanta, our church building was within the boundaries of the official Olympic village, and members worked hard to reach out formally to members of Parents, Families and Friends of Lesbians and Gays (PFLAG) and to members of other reconciling congregations.

In the past several months, through career changes and other matters unrelated to the reconciling issue, Trinity has lost several families who had provided major leadership and volunteer labor in ministries important to us. Obviously, those families will never be replaced. As Trinity stands at the door of this new life, questions face us. Are we at Trinity really being as welcoming as we need to be if we are to remain a strong and vocal voice for justice? Whom do we need to welcome? How do we reach these people and let them know what we stand for? How do we get them to stick around long enough to get to know us, and to get to be known by us? How do we continue to be God's people amidst the tangle of freeways and office buildings?

CHAPTER 9

First Congregational Church
Greenfield, Massachusetts

Shirlee M. Bromley, with Christine Trenholm

First Congregational Church is the oldest of the three Congregational churches in Greenfield, Massachusetts, a blue-collar town. The congregation was founded in the 1700s and had to relocate in the 1960s due to construction of an interstate highway. The move was extremely traumatic for the congregation. Before the demolition, the congregation had two ministers and two well-attended worship services. After the move, membership declined almost immediately. During the years I served as the congregation's pastor, average Sunday worship attendance was around 125. The church has the normal financial difficulties but also has a small endowment. During the week, a well-established nursery school with strong enrollment operates in the Sunday school rooms, and many young people have joined the church because of the nursery school. There are a few college degrees among the older members, but most of those under 45 have either attended or graduated from college.

Historically, First Congregational's reach in the community has been wide: The two other Congregational churches and the Unitarian church in Greenfield were all established from this congregation. Within the last 50 years, the church had a strong debate on the race issue (after not calling a black minister who was by far the most qualified of the congregation's candidates). In the last ten years, inclusive language and women in ordained ministry have been discussed as well. A strong majority of members has taken a more progressive stance on each of these issues, but there has also been underlying resentment from a few members.

The Decision to Talk about Homosexuality

Increased attention to homosexuality from the secular press, changes in human resources procedures by some community employers, and new state regulations for schools contributed to an increased awareness of homosexuality. People began to think about how the ideas they were hearing in the public arena fit with Christian teaching and tradition.

The catalyst for a study at First Congregational was a sermon I preached on the Beatitudes. I felt a need to speak about how blessed we are to know God, and that when we know our need of God we will stop hurting other people (especially gays, lesbians, and bisexuals, I was thinking). Before preaching, I announced that I would hold a sermon talk-back session, because I knew what I would be saying would be controversial. It was an emotional sermon for me because my partner and her daughter and son-in-law—my family—were in church that day. They did not know what I was planning to say. Although I did not come out as a lesbian directly in the sermon, one could easily read between the lines.

The talk-back session following worship was well attended. Eventually, someone asked about becoming an Open and Affirming (ONA) church: Were we one, and if not, why not? It was a very energizing meeting. A couple shared about their gay son, a woman about her gay brother, still others about gay or lesbian friends. Several people asked how we could go about studying this issue. The moderator of our church was present and helped us outline the process we would need to follow to undertake an ONA study.

A few days later and according to the congregation's by-laws, a formal request was made to the executive committee to appoint a chair and form an ad hoc committee to look at the ONA study. The executive council voted to begin the study and to extend an invitation to the entire congregation to participate. As soon as this was done, opposition raised its head—and never left!

Our Study Process

Announcements were made in the church bulletin, from the pulpit, and in the monthly newsletter inviting all who wished to study to participate. We used the ONA program of the United Church of Christ as our guide for the study and found it extremely helpful. Meetings were held twice a month. Additional speakers included a member of PFLAG, a lesbian minister, and someone from the local AIDS ministry. Videos from the UCC were used. The national press was full of stories and many of these were read and evaluated. There was an abundance of material available. Efforts were made to include all points of view and to try to come to an understanding of what was fact, myth, and relevant to the study. For example, the guidelines for the study suggested that congregations bring in someone to lead a discussion about the biblical passages that are problematic with regard to homosexuality. We invited a New Testament scholar and pastor who takes a sociocultural approach to the Bible. Those in opposition to the study were upset with this interpretation, so we brought in a conservative evangelical pastor and Bible teacher to present the other side. Unfortunately, this seemed only to make the rift wider.

We took our time with the study. As a matter of fact, our study lasted for nearly a year. More than 40 people participated, and the average attendance at study sessions was 30. We thought it was important that people's opinions be respected, and we let people know it was okay to attend the study and to oppose becoming an Opening and Affirming church. We hoped to provide an atmosphere where people could express their opinions and also listen to others.

Conflict as a Result of the Study

Throughout the process, the struggle within the church was immense. Much of the conflict seemed to revolve around one individual who had a history of being quite contrary. He was invited to the meetings and was listened to sympathetically by many people in the meetings but always went away angry. Finally, he became the symbolic leader for those who questioned the study. He made it his mission to stop the study and was supported by a long-time member, the articulate son of a former minister. Together they started a group that met outside the church, and about six months into the study, they called an all-church meeting to vote on ending the study. People in favor of the study were outraged that they might be denied the opportunity to explore this issue. The motion to end the study was defeated by ten votes, although the vote served as a signal that there were more than ten who opposed the study.

As a result of this meeting, the study was accelerated to let those who were upset know we were aware of their feelings and would finish our work as quickly as possible. A mediator from outside the church was also called in to listen to the grievances. No compromise could be reached, however. Those opposed to the study insisted it must be stopped, although by the time this point had been reached, the study was almost completed.

As the pastor I had a growing sense that I could no longer preach my convictions. Every sermon was seen by some to be about ONA, and some members feared our church was going to become a "gay" church. Though I would remain the pastor throughout the process, I tendered my resignation six weeks prior to the final vote on becoming an Open and Affirming congregation. After the vote, the moderator of the church also resigned. He had been viewed by some members as favoring ONA, even though he made every effort to moderate a very neutral and fair meeting.

In March 1994, the study culminated in writing an Open and Affirming statement. The whole study group discussed what should be in it, and then one member wrote it, knowing that it would be challenged by the study group and the congregation if presented. The study group made very few changes. After discussion about how to proceed, the group decided to call a church meeting and ask that a vote be taken.

The church meeting that was called to hear the ONA report and vote on becoming an ONA church was the best attended church meeting I have ever seen. People lined up outside the church sanctuary to sign in (they were required to declare they were active church members). Some reactivated their membership just to come and vote. Several neighboring pastors were there. The president and minister of the Massachusetts UCC Conference was there as well as the associate conference minister of our area. It was an impassioned meeting to the end. ONA passed by 11 votes. The opposition also introduced a motion that the church withdraw its membership from the UCC. This motion was soundly defeated. Finally, the study group voted to declare the study finished and quietly live with the statement.

In Hindsight

It always helps to have hindsight. I think the study would have gone better if the church leaders had more effectively dealt with the one person who made it clear from the beginning that he was unhappy with the process. In the beginning, the study group tried to be patient and receptive to him, but that became increasingly difficult. Edwin Friedman once said that if you have a tiger in your midst, you should either cage or destroy him, and no one knew how to do that. I think it is important to note that this man and his wife, who had a good deal of power in the church, had lost their son to suicide two years before. At the time of the tragedy, they readily lent themselves to my pastoring. Still, they had been somewhat stoic about the death until the ONA study came up, and then all their anger began to come out.

Since the study, the chairperson of the study has said she wishes that as the opposition began to assemble, she had found the time to meet privately with the ten people and to listen to them individually, not to argue but to work toward the idea that the well-being of the church was more important than one issue and that one's sexual orientation was a matter between that person and God. She believes there must have been a way to stop the polarization, but she could not find it. Perhaps first studying sexuality in general would have helped.

It should also be mentioned that during the time of the study and just after it, the custodian who was very much appreciated by the congregation died, the associate pastor left and the position was not filled for financial reasons, and the organist and choir director of over 20 years retired. Two secretaries also retired, and the director of the nursery school left to take another position in public education. Then I resigned. Although the death and resignations were unrelated to the study, the lack of familiar leaders did make the congregation's healing after the vote more difficult.

The congregation as a whole probably learned they are pretty representative of the population of the United States. Many in the church have indicated they learned and benefited from the experience, even if they did not attend meetings but only asked for the handouts. Those who supported the study, however, have all said they have never regretted the process. Several have stated they had no idea what homosexuality was, and they believe they now have a better understanding of what the fuss was all about and why biblical interpretations could be confusing. They thought the education and increased awareness about homosexuality was invaluable and that they are better people for having gone through the study. Individual members indicated they developed a stronger understanding of the Bible, their personal relationship to God, and the role of the church in forming, shaping, and living of Christian lives. They learned that there can be honest and valid differences in how we react to current issues.

There is no question some people felt left out of the conversation. Once the polarization set in, there did not seem to be a way to bridge the divisions. Most of those who supported becoming an ONA church have now left First Congregational and have become involved in churches in other towns. The church now has a new pastor, and he has declared a moratorium on the subject. The congregation is smaller, the minister is part-time, and Sunday school enrollment was four at the beginning of this year. There is a common understanding that the issue of homosexuality is not to be mentioned, although other minorities receive regular attention. The recently called minister left the words "homosexuals, gays, and lesbians" off the list of those whom the church embraces, but race, gender, and so forth were mentioned.

When I reflect on the process, I feel proud of the people who were willing to risk and take leadership in the midst of such adversity. Encouraging members to participate in the discussion, ensuring the meetings held in the church parlor had an air of openness, fostering an atmosphere of wanting to learn and study, establishing guidelines for listening, beginning each study session with a prayer asking for help to understand one another, and ending each meeting with the opportunity for each person to express a thought or feelings from the session were all wise and helpful steps.

At the same time, I still feel some sadness and anger about the terrible divisiveness that erupted. Distance and time have brought healing to me and, I hope, for the church. Though difficult and painful, I do not regret having taken the church through the study. The experience enabled me to take some new risks and to move on to more openness and freedom in my own life and ministry.

The unfortunate thing is that I also learned that when the congregation could not resolve its differences, it followed the pattern of the past. First one group withheld it pledges, then the second group almost entirely left the church. Each complicated social change has been difficult for the church, and each time it has hesitated, it has lost members. Some of the leaders who were opposed to blacks have now openly stated they had been wrong on that issue, and the church has finally accepted a minister of another race. But in general, the congregation has not learned how to have differences of opinion and tolerate—let alone be open to and affirm—those who hold different views.

In reflection, I wonder if such a study might not be generally more effective if there are gays and lesbians already in the church who are willing to step forward. I felt that if I were to come out, I would split the church right then and there. I was not willing to do that, because I had served the congregation for nearly eight years and was already feeling it was time for me to move on. Had I come out, it would have been important for me to stay and see the healing through.

Perhaps it is most telling that the study chairperson, who is still a member of the congregation, has indicated she would like to be a member of a group and undertake the rigors of study on another difficult topic. She believes study groups are an important part of church life in that they help us apply our faith to today's issues. They make us think. She would even volunteer to help get the study materials together!

CHAPTER 10

Edina Community Lutheran Church

Edina, Minnesota

Pamela Johnson

Who Are We?

Edina Community Lutheran Church (Evangelical Lutheran Church in America) was founded in 1948 in a first-ring suburb of Minneapolis. Minnesota is often called the Mecca of Lutheranism, so members of our congregation drive by many other Lutheran churches to get to Edina Community. Part of what has attracted people to the congregation during the last 50 years is its long history of social activism and demonstrated leadership in issues of justice. Members of the congregation were very active during the civil rights movement of the 1960s, including marching with Dr. Martin Luther King Jr. and standing with the Native American community at Wounded Knee, South Dakota. In the 1970s Edina Community called Barb Andrews, one of the first woman pastors in the Lutheran church, and was among the early congregations to become Reconciled in Christ, in May 1985.[1] We currently have an average worship attendance of 220 with a good mix of ages and genders but a very limited class and racial mix, with the majority of the congregation being of middle-class, European heritage.

My family joined Edina Community in 1984. It struck us almost immediately that this is a group of people who can talk well together. It is not a community that always agrees, but it is a community that *practices* respectful listening, and I think this is a key to our growth as an inclusive community.

Why Did We Start Talking?

In the early 1980s the congregation began a planning and visioning process whose outcome was a mission purpose statement. Our congregation is led by a council of ministers (the minister of education, the minister of evangelism, the minister of mission, and so forth). Each ministry has various standing and task-oriented committees. When the visioning process began, each ministry focused on discerning the mission and purpose of our life together as a faith community. In addition, we gathered the entire congregation for several evening and Saturday meetings in which we talked about how we intended to live together and how we could best articulate our collective mission.

The following is the result of that year-long process.

Mission/Purpose Statement
of Edina Community Lutheran Church
Adopted by the Congregation on January 15, 1985

Edina Community Lutheran Church is a community of people baptized into Christ. Through God's grace we struggle corporately and individually to live, grow, and develop as Christ's followers through worship, confession, forgiveness, service, advocacy, study, mutual support, and peacemaking.

To pursue and fulfill this mission we agree:

- to worship regularly and inclusively as a gathered community, around Word and Sacrament;
- to witness, as redeemed persons whose lives have been fulfilled with God's grace and who are called to invite all others to share in that grace;
- to serve, in Christ's name, working to bring healing to the brokenness and separation in our lives and in society;
- to study, sharing critical inquiry as we grow in understanding of God's will for our lives, and the life of the world, and to meet new challenges and gain new perspectives on our faith;
- to advocate mercy, justice, liberation, and peacemaking in our lives, communities, nation, and the world, committing ourselves to

nonviolence in all relationships, striving to increase awareness of issues of hunger, oppression, war, and peace;

- to care for one another, to resolve conflict with love, honesty, directness, openness, and gentleness, and to support those in need beyond our community, affirming that all persons are created in God's image to be whole and to be treated with respect and dignity;
- to encourage one another to witness and serve in our daily lives by developing and using our gifts, time, money, and resources, inviting all persons to share in God's grace;
- to support ministries in our community, work cooperatively with other churches and organizations, and through benevolence giving, with the programs of the Minneapolis Area Synod and the Evangelical Lutheran Church in America;
- to welcome all persons, without regard to sex, marital status, age, race, sexual orientation, abilities, or other human conditions, inviting all into membership, mission, and leadership.

This grassroots visioning process was key to our becoming Reconciled in Christ. The statement contains many commitments to inclusivity and lays out a covenant of mutual respect that welcomes all people into membership, mission, and leadership. The statement was so clear about welcoming people without regard to sex, marital status, age, race, sexual orientation, abilities, or other human conditions that our council of ministers voted, unanimously and without debate, to have our congregation become a Reconciled in Christ congregation, openly declaring the congregation's invitation to gay and lesbian membership and leadership. The council of ministers did not expect what happened next.

What Did We Learn?

The first thing we learned is that even in a culture that prides itself on respectful listening, certain viewpoints might feel silenced. The wave of agreement about language of inclusiveness had prevented some people from saying they did not think inclusivity was such a good idea. And the wave of agreement kept us from really having the kind of frank, specific conversation we needed to have before publicly declaring ourselves a welcoming community to gay and lesbian people. Some people who had previously been silent now raised very big questions about homosexuality: theological questions arising out of biblical texts and practical questions about how this new openness would affect the composition and nature of our community.

The second thing we learned is that expediency can ignite unseen resentment. The council of ministers had, in all good faith, made a forthright and expedient decision that they believed was a natural outgrowth of our grassroots visioning. Ironically, their decision led us to the conversation we needed.

The third thing we learned is that people interpret words differently. We had not collectively unpeeled the onion of inclusivity. We assumed too much without fully exploring what each of us thought it meant to be an inclusive community.

How Did We Go Forward?

The council of ministers was surprised that questions were raised about our being a Reconciled in Christ congregation. When they realized that the congregation needed to talk specifically about issues of homosexuality, they devised a process of two adult forums followed by a congregational meeting.

The first adult forum addressed the biblical and theological questions, seeking to understand what the Bible has to say about homosexuality and why. Both our pastor and laypeople led and participated in this discussion, giving background to specific passages and interpreting those passages in the larger context of the Gospel.[2] In retrospect this forum was necessary and fruitful, but it was the second adult forum that was a turning point in our congregation's understanding of gay and lesbian people and the issues of oppression they face.

The second forum was a panel of our own members. Panel members for the first time courageously shared with us that they were gay themselves, or that they were the parent or brother or sister of a gay or lesbian person. This was an enormously powerful and moving experience. Panel members talked about the struggle to live ordinary lives as they were confronted by injustice, fear, and open abuse. They talked about the joys of ordinary life surrounded by the love of friends and the beauty of the earth. In short, they confirmed that all people are created in God's image.

The response to that panel was both overwhelming support and a "coming to a head" of anger and fear. One panel member has since shared with me that a member of the congregation who was against being Reconciled in Christ caught him after the panel and said that he was angry and frustrated and really could not take any more of this talk about homosexuality. Years later that person has apologized for his words at the time. But the gift of the panel was that it allowed people to speak their genuine and heartfelt fear as well as their support. It seemed to clear the way for an authentic conversation at our congregational meeting.

The congregational meeting was very well attended. The purpose of the meeting was clearly stated. We were there to either affirm or repeal the council of ministers' decision to declare our congregation a Reconciled in Christ congregation. People spoke respectfully and passionately. I remember how deeply we probed the question of what it means to be inclusive when one member asked, "Does being inclusive mean that we would welcome a pedophile or a necrophile into our membership and leadership?" Although his question revealed his perception of homosexuality as a deviant behavior, he was not asking a question about degrees of deviance. He was rather asking us to truly decide whether we meant *all* people would be welcomed into our community of faith. After both silence and speech, we decided that we would not draw a line where we believed God does not. We then truly knew what we meant by being an inclusive community, and the council of ministers' decision was affirmed.

It may still be difficult for some members of our congregation to accept our decision to be Reconciled in Christ. But we are generally a congregation that knows how to talk well together and then how to let the decisions reached go forward without second guessing, without bitterness. Over time very few families have left our community because of various decisions with which they were not comfortable.

What Has Being Reconciled in Christ Meant for Our Community?

I asked several members of our community this question. Here are some of their answers:

- "We have been richly blessed by the talented, grace-filled people who have joined our congregation because we are Reconciled in Christ. Gay and lesbian people have revived our spirit, leading us in worship, preaching, teaching, and opening opportunities to do justice."
- "Young people in our midst who are gay or lesbian feel a lot less isolated."
- "A ministry of friendship has been cemented between some of our gay members and some of the elderly members of our community."
- "My picture of what a family looks like has been expanded and enriched. When we first came and saw a church directory with two men in a family picture, I knew I had found the right church!"
- "Being the parents of a lesbian daughter who lives 2,000 miles away, I've loved getting to know other young people who are gay or lesbian. Here I can feel free to talk about our daughter's commitment ceremony and pass around pictures of that wonderful event in her and our lives."
- "I have grown in the realization that lesbian and gay couples are partners in a sacred, committed marriage just as I am."
- "I've really come full circle. At one time I'd thought of being Reconciled in Christ as a justice issue, and I believed Edina Community should make a statement. Now I see it as simply being with all God's people."
- "It's been important to me that we keep all voices in the mix. If gay people didn't talk to straight people and include them in our lives and activities, we'd be diminished."
- "I appreciate having a community where I'm able to be openly part of a couple and talk about what my partner and I do for a living or what our plans are for the future or all we went through to have our baby."
- "Children learn by sensing and seeing. Our community's children are blessed to have gay and lesbian people in their lives. When

they're 17 and someone says, 'Now let's discuss the issue of homosexuality,' they'll know from their own experience it's not an issue,
it's simply faithful people living faithful lives."
- "Edina Community welcomes us as whole people of faith—not as
  lesbian people. It's the first place where we as partners are a family
  and our picture appears together in the church directory. There's
  something going on—the welcoming has to do with actually bringing all people into leadership. It is a place where Paul's words, 'in
  Christ there is neither Jew nor Greek,' are lived out in ordinary, pro-
  gressive-supper, read-the-lessons, chat-about-the-weekend ways."

Final Thoughts

I think there are four key elements to our growth individually and collectively as a welcoming, inclusive community. The first key is that we
approached the question of inclusivity wholistically. We looked at welcoming gay and lesbian people within the context of welcoming all
people. As part of our visioning process, we asked ourselves the question, How do we want to live together? I think it is significant that in our
mission/purpose statement we have the words "we agree." This helps us
remember that we have made promises to each other that *we will* worship inclusively and *we will* witness to and welcome all people. This
will, this resolve to be an inclusive community, is now a natural part of
our fabric.

The second key element is that the desire to be a welcoming community must be held jointly by the clergy and the lay leadership. Either
the clergy or the laity can initiate the conversation, but they must struggle *together* through the theological, social, and personal issues that
arise. If one side of the leadership is dragging the other, the community
will suffer rather than flourish.

A third key for us was to invite gay and lesbian people into *leadership* in the congregation. One of our first gay members took on the
daunting task of chairing the building fund committee! This is a community in which everyone can sit in the pew and they can also preach and
celebrate the Sacraments. Everyone is encouraged to teach, chair a
ministry, sing, share their abilities, try new tasks.

A fourth and final key for our community has been to embrace a blessing. I do not think we had any idea in 1985 how God would bless our community by the simple act of our saying, "Come in, you are welcome here." Daily we are shaken awake, encouraged, given tea and toast, challenged and enriched by God, each other, and our mission together.

CHAPTER 11

Brookmeade Congregational Church, United Church of Christ

Nashville, Tennessee

Daniel Rosemergy

The Brookmeade Congregational Church, UCC, is a progressive, liberal congregation in the "buckle of the Bible Belt." Its history includes being a leader in the civil rights era and assisting in the integration of Nashville in the 1960s. It is a small urban church of 160 members and friends with an average worship attendance of approximately 65. The congregation is highly educated, diverse in age, with a fairly transient membership. The membership includes five ordained UCC ministers, in addition to the full-time pastor, who are in various special ministries in the city. The congregation is a teaching parish of the Vanderbilt University Divinity School.

The weekly Sunday worship bulletin includes this summary of our mission:

> Brookmeade is an Open and Affirming, inclusive, and a Just Peace church committed to spiritual growth and the struggle for peace and social justice in our lives and in society. Our religious language is guided by an inclusive language policy in all references to persons and in seeking diversity of images and metaphors in re-ferring to God.

The Journey

Our journey began in the mid-1980s when the congregation offered to be matched with a congregation of the predominantly homosexual Metropolitan Community Church (MCC) in a city-wide pulpit exchange, which involved exchange of pastors and mutual congregational participation in the other's faith education program and worship. Our congregants had the opportunity to come to know a large number of people from all walks of life who happened to be gay or lesbian, many of whom were in long-term covenantal relationships. A number of MCC members asked to be on our mailing list and have often attended church activities over the years. In addition, I was invited to provide emergency pastoral care for MCC when their own pastor was away from the city.

Also at that time, our church was one of the early supporters of Nashville CARES, an educational and support service organization for people who are HIV-positive, or who have AIDS, and their families. We provided space for CARES volunteer training, family support groups, and a range of other activities. We also developed a six-week educational program on HIV/AIDS for our own congregation to provide accurate information and to allay any fears about having people with AIDS in the church.

All of this combined to create a welcoming atmosphere for gays and lesbians, and during the mid- to late-1980s, a significant number—some out, others not—joined the church. Brookmeade generally is not a judgmental or pushy place, and people are not pressed to share personal information until they wish to do so. Thus a person's sexual orientation simply did not matter for a vast majority of the congregation. As a result of this general climate of openness, however, whenever someone raised the subject of formally beginning a study and discussion process to determine whether we wanted to declare ourselves an Open and Affirming congregation, the response was often, "We already are. Why start something that could be divisive?" And so we continued into the early 1990s without holding formal discussions.

In retrospect, I believe that was a mistake. Underneath what seemed to be a tranquil acceptance of gays and lesbians in our congregation, there were a few members who were deeply concerned about their presence in the congregation. But these concerned members did not openly share their feelings. And more important, we had not clearly said that being Open and Affirming was an important part of who we were as a church. So some gay and lesbian members wondered whether they really were welcome and whether we would affirm them in all their life experiences (as partners, when they celebrated anniversaries or suffered the pain of separations, as they sought employment and housing). And we were not standing in solidarity with the other (relatively few) UCC congregations who had formally declared themselves as ONA churches during the mid- to late-1980s. Then two things happened.

The Challenge

I was invited to serve as a panelist along with William Sloane Coffin (who was a scholar in residence at the Vanderbilt University Divinity School at the time) in a discussion titled "The Church and Homosexuality." In the course of this discussion, I stated that Brookmeade was "in fact" Open and Affirming, even though we had not formally declared that we were. Following the event, the Rev. Coffin pulled me aside and said, "Dan, I'm not going to let you get away with that again. You're *not* an 'Open and Affirming' congregation until you give the congregation an opportunity to study, discuss, and search their hearts and vote finally to state clearly—out of their faith convictions—that they are an Open and Affirming congregation and that they will live out that covenant in all that they are and do." That challenge gnawed at me in the weeks following the conversation.

At about that time, the congregation decided to undertake a long-range planning process. The beginning step was a comprehensive congregational survey form that members were invited to complete about the church, their sense of the state of the church, their dreams and their concerns. I was taken aback but not totally surprised when two or three people wrote about how deeply troubled they were about the gays and lesbians in our congregation, suggesting they were not "normal" and were "seriously hurting the possible growth of the church." All written responses to the survey were compiled, printed, and distributed to members. Along with most members of the church, I was offended by these remarks. We all realized that now was the time to undertake a study and discussion process that would lead to a congregational vote on whether or not we were and would be an Open and Affirming church.

The Process

The challenge was put on the agenda of our board of deacons, a five-member board responsible for the spiritual well-being of our congregation, worship and sacraments, shared pastoral care of members, and outreach ministries. At the time its members included a retired laywoman (chair), a retired male UCC minister, a laywoman nurse, a laywoman attorney, and a layman social worker who was openly gay. I met with them, asking them to take the leadership in guiding the congregation through this process. I would be supportive, provide resources, and be available to all congregants, but I did not want to be perceived as "pushing" the process through, although it was clear to the congregation where I stood on the issue.

The board of deacons took the challenge seriously. They held extensive discussions over several meetings about the congregation's readiness, the importance and implications of undertaking such a conversation, and possible resources (materials and people) to assist them. They voted unanimously to accept the responsibility to develop a proposal and process to submit to the church council and subsequently to the entire congregation.

When preparing for their work, the deacons decided to do two preliminary things. First, they consulted with and obtained resource materials from the Rev. Ann Day, coordinator of the Open and Affirming Program in the UCC. They received voluminous materials, including a 55-minute color VHS video (and printed guides), "Open and Affirming: A Journey of Faith." The video documents the experience of three UCC congregations going through the Open and Affirming process. The deacons also had the opportunity to meet personally with the Rev. Day on one of her visits to Nashville.

Second, after careful review of the materials, they decided to undertake the study and discussion process as a group of five. (I was invited but decided not to attend so as not to influence them.) They had originally questioned whether they should do this, because they were all in favor of becoming an Open and Affirming church. They decided, however, to proceed so they would be familiar with the materials, issues, and questions that arose, and could identify potential problems. They discovered, in addition, that each of them, coming from different backgrounds and current understandings, had differing perspectives, questions, feelings, and thoughts that the process both engendered and provided a way to deal with. It was all extremely helpful in their development of a study process proposal.

As a part of their study-process, they wrote the initial draft of a possible covenant statement. The statement said in part:

In addition to the commandment to love God, we recognize God's inclusive love for us as a gift to love and be loved by others. We are called to work together in the light of the Gospel to define principles of human relationships and behavior that are based on relating to all persons as children of God, with love, responsibility, accountability, trust, and mutual nurture.... Therefore, we welcome people of all sexual orientations to join our congregation in the same spirit and manner used in the acceptance of any new members.

It was at this time that process facilitators decided to talk privately with all those in the congregation whom the process facilitators knew were gay or lesbian. Facilitators asked these members for their thoughts about the process and invited their participation at whatever level they were comfortable. Leaders made it clear that there was no expectation about the role they would or would not play.

At the end of their own study process, the board of deacons developed a proposal for a comprehensive educational study and discussion schedule to present to the church council. The council discussed the proposal at great length over the course of two meetings, weighing the pros and cons and wrestling with concerns about dividing the congregation, losing members, losing pledged income, becoming known as a "gay" church," and so forth. (It should be noted that none of these things happened.) After all voices had been heard, the council voted unanimously to proceed and to ask the congregation's approval to undertake the study-process. The congregational meeting discussion echoed the council discussion but ended with a vote to proceed. The deacons were charged with the responsibility of guiding the process.

The board sent a letter to all congregants summarizing the process to date and the study and discussion schedule. The schedule of sharing opportunities included:

- a noon potluck and viewing of the video "Opening and Affirming: A Journey of Faith," followed by discussion;
- presentations and discussion in two separate sessions, "Being an Open and Affirming Church: Theological and Ethical Issues for Our Faith" and "Biblical Perspectives on Homosexuality: What the Bible Does and Doesn't Say";
- a supper and program with a pastor of an Open and Affirming

church who is himself openly gay;

- a discussion session with representatives of the UCC Parents of Lesbians and Gays.

At some point during these sessions, several members of the congregation said they felt the need for time as a community simply to talk, share feelings, ask questions, and express concerns and hopes—without presenters, guests, and specific program topics. The response to the suggestion was enthusiastic, and so the deacons scheduled a separate evening to come together "without agenda." It turned out to be the most significant part of the process.

The deacons asked the church moderator, a long-time and respected church member, to guide the meeting, and they asked a young clergywoman and pastoral counselor (a member of Brookmeade) to help facilitate and process feelings and disagreements, and to be a calming presence if tensions or deep emotions flared. It was the best-attended session of the process, and following initial hesitancy on the part of some, folks began to take risks, openly sharing with the group some deep and emotional questions about homosexuality and bisexuality, and fears about the implications for the church. Questions and feelings were dealt with openly, honestly, and with respect and love from the facilitators and others in the group. Two members, one gay and the other lesbian, spoke openly for the first time about their sexual orientation and told their stories, including their experiences at Brookmeade and in the wider community. One young woman, a lesbian in a long-time committed relationship with a woman who was also a member of the church, subsequently asked for time to give a "Moment of Sharing" during our Sunday worship to tell her story. A number of people created other opportunities for follow-up discussion, such as counseling with the pastor about issues of their own sexuality.

A large percentage of the congregation participated in the study programs and discussion. The deacons used periodic update articles in the church newsletter, worship bulletin announcements, and regular reports to church leaders on ways to focus congregational attention on the ongoing process and to encourage continued participation. In addition, the deacons decided it was important to make personal contact with people we had not seen at the study sessions and the few people we knew were against our undertaking the process leading to a vote. A list was compiled and one of three people—myself as pastor, the clergywoman pastoral counselor, or a layman who is a clinical psychologist—was assigned to make contact with the congregant. The purpose of the contacts, which included phone calls, brief in-person conversations at other church functions, or visits, was simply to say, "We're interested in your views and feelings. You're an important part of this community, and we want to hear and respond to your thoughts." We offered additional information and resources for their use, additional discussion times, or personal meetings to assist them. The responses to our initiatives varied, but people were always grateful we cared enough to ask. A few folks did take advantage of the opportunity to discuss their feelings and thoughts on a one-on-one basis, rather than in a group setting.

We started all sessions and conversations by inviting people to express openly and to share their thoughts and by explaining that we welcome diverse opinions and points of view. We asked that everyone listen to others with respect and love. Fortunately, our congregation has a long history of open and honest discussion on a wide range of issues.

The Decision

The congregational vote to become an Open and Affirming congregation seemed almost anticlimactic. The specially called meeting was well attended, and the spirit was clearly positive. The deacons' motion that we formally adopt the revised Covenant Declaring Ourselves an Open and Affirming Congregation was greeted with a chorus of seconds. Discussion was thoughtful, balanced, and brief. Prior to the meeting, the council had agreed that the vote would be by written ballot and that members could vote in absentia. Voice or hand votes are the norm in our congregation, but in this instance we thought a private ballot ensured that individuals could vote without any fear of peer pressure. The vote was overwhelmingly positive, with just a few no votes and abstentions.

We did not lose any members as a result of this decision. In fact, those who had publicly expressed their opposition continue as active members of the congregation and have not only accepted the congregational decision but have helped us live out the covenant in numerous ways. For example, we have had unanimous support in our efforts to reach out to gays and lesbians in our community and to become more welcoming. Even seemingly little things such as including the names of our gay and lesbian members' partners in our congregational directory have been recognized as important and have been broadly supported.

The Open and Affirming Committee

The deacons, with council approval, decided to create an ongoing Open and Affirming committee to guide our life together as an ONA congregation. The reality of that statement has been reflected in the activities and commitments of the church since. Our statement that we are an ONA church appears each Sunday in the worship bulletin, and copies of the covenant are on display in the church lobby and are used in new member information sessions. We have revised church forms to accommodate information about a partner as well as a spouse, and we have changed the church directory, listing partners together. We advertise regularly in the area gay and lesbian newspapers and are participants each year in gay pride events in Nashville. We are developing church library resources on related issues and plan to sponsor a roundtable with other Open and Affirming congregations in the area. The excitement and enthusiasm of our ONA committee is contagious within the congregation. The committee chairperson said, "ONA for us is not just a declared and written statement. It is a way we live our faith. It is a way of service, support, and even evangelism as we say clearly that all God's children are worthy, valued, affirmed, and welcome in this community."

Reflection on the Experience

I am persuaded that the process itself, regardless of the issue, has changed the congregation. In fact, the opportunity for all members to share in developing and discussing the covenant statement and to come together in open and honest discussions made us a closer and more loving congregation, with a deeper sense of our faith and what it means to live in the world. To be sure, differences were expressed but always with respect for others, and there was more hugging than we had seen for some time. And dealing with one another with a sense of respect, love, and caring continues to be a part of who we are as a congregation. We are a closer community, more honest with ourselves and one another.

We have a new sense of mission, not just with gays and lesbians but in a wide range of areas, such as homelessness, poverty, the environment. And we have experienced in a new way the importance of intentional and covenantal work together. The process itself helped us understand how to create community and live out our faith day to day, how to move from talking about our faith to living it. Our covenantal work has become an expression of who and what we are as a church.

When looking back, I realize how fortunate we were to have such visionary, courageous, and sensitive lay leadership who so carefully developed a proposal with broad-based input and who guided the process to include all congregants. They created opportunities and a safe setting for full and honest sharing and dialogue, and emphasized the importance of respecting differing points of view and being committed to whatever the community decision would be. I am proud of this church and what we are becoming in God's spirit as an ONA congregation.

PART 3

What Works?

CHAPTER 12

Constructive Conflict or Harmonious Dishonesty?

Donald E. Bossart

Seven case studies of churches that have taken on the task of studying homosexuality have been submitted for analysis to learn what is helpful and what is not in such a process. A brief summary of each case follows in order to provide the reader with background for the analysis that concludes this chapter.

First Congregational Church of Fresno

This is an old, central-city congregation known for its liberal standing in a conservative region. It is a 500-member church, larger than the other study churches. The congregation was once larger but has declined, some feel because of its social action over the years. It is now growing, and some members are fearful that controversy would disrupt that growth. The two pastors became involved in gay and lesbian ministry and ministry with people with AIDS, leading to a felt need to bring the congregation into that ministry. The pastors understood the ministry as one of relating to the neighborhood around the church. The church council was receptive to a study and discernment about homosexuality, so a study group was formed to meet monthly. This group planned a churchwide study and discernment process that might lead to a decision that the congregation declare itself Open and Affirming. The church council authorized the study and appointed an ONA task force. The announcement of the task force's formation in the church newsletter led to some resistance among members, because it appeared to some that war was being declared.

Educational forums were held. Open sessions for dialogue allowed members to express feelings of fear and of hope. Some members thought the congregation's self-image as an inclusive community was challenged by this study. Other participants wondered why homosexuality was singled out for study. A psychologist held a special session on biomedical information addressing the question of whether homosexuality is a matter of choice or genetics. Two seminar series were led by the pastors on ethical and biblical themes.

Finally, the congregation voted on an ONA statement, which was accepted with an 84 percent majority. The threat of conflict with its attending anxiety was experienced and weathered. The bonds of members' mutual respect showed they could endure conflict and enjoy change and new insights. Members' experience with gays and lesbians showed them that these people were in need of ministry, and members therefore invested them-selves in such ministries. Actual growth in the congregation resulted from this experience and decision.

Dayton Avenue Presbyterian Church

This is a small, racially diverse, urban congregation with a very high level of commitment. It is open to the neighborhood, and its diversity is a characteristic identified by those who choose membership. The congregation has a long history of community involvement and social justice ministry. These are critical aspects of this case study.

The social action committee of Dayton Avenue Presbyterian Church recommended a study to the session in response to the denomination's request that the congregation engage in dialogue on the issue of human sexuality and church leadership. Two groups within the congregation said a study was not needed. One of these groups said the Bible's teachings against homosexuality were clear, and the other group said the church was already committed against injustice, so no extra effort was needed. Most members were uncommitted and were somewhat reluctant to open discussion. Fear of conflict was definitely present. The session made a one-year commitment to study, and the social-action committee then became responsible for that exploration and conversation. The plan included the following:

- Listening to members' concerns at four all-church forums
- Bringing in outside educational resource people
- Holding several multi-week adult education classes
- Showing videos borrowed from denominational resources
- Focusing worship services on this theme
- Holding small group discussions among every identifiable small group within the congregation
- Training group discussion leaders

Important attempts were made to be as inclusive as possible. Ground rules were established based on denominational principles (mutual forbearance toward those who disagree). The session finally adopted a statement of openness and affirmation and presented it to the congregation, and the statement was adopted. Some members did not agree with the decision but nonetheless accepted it. No loss of members resulted.

The turning point was when the issue became personal to some in the congregation. Failure to minister to a member's gay son led to prayers. Stories were lifted up as crucial for the ministry among the congregation's diverse members and neighbors. Many experienced a deepening of their own personal faith as a result of their work on this issue.

The congregation's pastor learned that members needed to know and honor each other's personal, familial, and theological history in order to honor and respect differences of opinion. He also learned that it was a mistake to assume members knew anything about homosexuality or the traditional church position on homosexuality, and that all members needed to have balanced information from the biblical, medical, and sociological fields. Time lines would also have helped the discussions. More small-group involvement and reporting to the whole church would also have helped. Recognition of God's mission, which is beyond our differences, was deemed paramount for the process. Development of trust in small groups was felt to be crucial. A consequence of the endeavor was that interest in biblical and theological learning increased.

Zion United Church of Christ

The context out of which a congregation discusses homosexuality makes a great deal of difference. Zion UCC describes itself as an intentional community committed to inclusive evangelism.

The congregation's self-image is that members want to reach out and receive people "as they are." The pastor leader, as a gay person, was definitely committed to the congregation's declaring itself an Open and Affirming congregation and recognized that the congregation's sense of mission and commitment to justice and peace issues also related to being Open and Affirming.

Several helpful processes already used by Zion were particularly helpful during their study and decision time. Members of the congregation signed an annual written covenant that focused them on the centrality of their life and work in the community. They used a consensus style of decision making for their congregational work. And this unique congregation drew from a very large radius around Henderson, Kentucky, and had a reputation for service and commitment to diversity. This congregational background provides a clue about the likely outcome of the study. The pastor's leadership was another significant factor: he continually held before the congregation a vision for the church and was a loving and effective pastor as a gay person.

A patient, step-by-step process was used to initiate the study of homosexuality. A basic leadership team was established for the process. The study involved the whole church organization, not just a select group. The congregation's self-image was of being open, but the members wisely understood the human tendency to harbor some prejudices. To address this self-understanding, they planned a churchwide conversation with professional facilitators to help people talk about their feelings and ask questions about homosexuality. The facilitators' reports helped the church focus on its particular need. A strong educational program emerged from the information provided by the congregational conversation. Continual opportunity was provided for church members to express their feelings about the process and the subject. The leadership team exhibited an unhurried thoroughness.

Extended listening, total involvement, a consensus decisionmaking process, and a vision with which to identify played a central role in Zion's completion of a successful study. The context of their congregational commitment to being an intentional community as well as one focused on justice and peace is basic to their study and vote to declare themselves Open and Affirming.

Trinity United Methodist Church

This old, inner-city congregation historically played a significant role in Atlanta. Trinity gave birth to many other congregations and had a reputation as a leader in the fight for civil rights. More recently, the congregation has established a strong ministry to the homeless and people who are HIV-positive or who have AIDS. At the same time, however, after several decades of decreasing membership, the congregation is the beneficiary of financial support from other congregations.

Trinity's story differs from others in this book in that homosexuality became an issue not so much through an individual but because of the actions of organizations. A request from the Atlanta Gay Men's Chorus to hold auditions and rehearsals in Trinity's building resulted in some painful, unsuccessful negotiations that surfaced tensions around homosexuality. But it was the work of a group of Methodist clergy who call themselves the "Confessing Movement" that really sparked conversation within the congregation. This group disseminated a document called the "Houston Declaration," which among other things opposed homosexual practice. In response, members of Trinity developed and endorsed a "Call for Renewal" that was also endorsed by Methodists across the country.

When the congregation discovered that their Call for Renewal was in essence a Reconciling Congregation statement, members began to discuss the issue of homosexuality in Sunday school classes and other forums. The congregation is now officially a Reconciling Congregation and members are seeking ways to put that status into action.

First Congregational Church

Membership at the time of the study was about 250, and First Congregational Church was the oldest UCC congregation in town, but it had been demolished and rebuilt because of a new highway. There was a liberal tendency in the congregation but also a conservative segment. Race, inclusive language, and women in ministry had become issues. The self-image of the congregation was not that of an inclusive community or social justice congregation.

The decision to study about homosexuality came as a result of the larger community's involvement with the issue of inclusiveness, plus a sermon talk-back session with the pastor. A study group was convened as a result of the interest shown at the talk-back. Standard congregational procedures were used to set up the study.

A critical decision was made by the study leadership and the pastors. An open invitation was made through the church newsletter to invite all interested to come and participate. The resulting group met twice a month. Good resources were selected for use, including the denomination's study materials and local resources on biblical questions, members of PFLAG, (Parents, Families and Freinds of Lesbians and Gays), AIDS ministry, and a lesbian minister. A group of about ten tried to stop the study but was not successful. The study concluded with the writing of an ONA statement that was submitted to the whole congregation for acceptance. The word *affirming* was a stumbling block, but the statement passed by ten votes. A mediator was used to try to work with the opposition, but no compromise resulted. Pledges were held back and some left the church. Still, those members who participated in the study group felt they grew as a result of the study.

Edina Community Lutheran Church

This church is in a first-ring suburb of Minneapolis and has attracted members because of its leadership in social concerns. The church has a history of members being able to talk with each other respectfully.

A planning and visioning process begun in the early 1980s resulted in the development of a mission purpose statement. This is a critical part of the context for this congregation's study of homosexuality. A commitment to study and to heal brokenness led to members' intention for inclusiveness. As a result, the church council announced its decision to have the congregation become a Reconciled in Christ congregation.

This announcement sparked resentment and concern that this new, formal status would affect the nature of the community. The expedient action of the church council had revealed unprocessed feelings, and the public nature of this welcome to the gay and lesbian community angered and frightened members. This outcome from the visioning process led to the conversations that were now needed.

This need to talk led to two forums followed by a congregational meeting. Biblical and theological questions were dealt with in the first forum. The second one was the turning point. It involved a panel of members who were gay or lesbian or who were related to gays or lesbians. Their struggles became personal to the membership, resulting in some members feeling supportive, a counterpoint to the feelings of anger and fear felt by other members. More heartfelt talk was the result. The congregational meeting that concluded the process was very open and well attended. Members decided that they would not draw lines where God did not, affirming their inclusive community designation as a Reconciled in Christ congregation.

The following elements in the process were essential:

- The welcoming of gay and lesbian people was viewed wholistically—as an aspect of the commitment to inclusiveness of all people.
- The welcoming community was understood to require both clergy and lay leadership.
- Gays and lesbians were invited to be leaders within the congregation.
- The inclusiveness was felt to be a blessing to the congregation.

Brookmeade Congregational Church

This is a progressive, liberal congregation in the Bible Belt of Nashville, Tennessee. It has a history of leading in the civil rights era and integration of Nashville. The congregation is small, and members are highly educated, diverse, and transient. Brookmeade is a teaching parish of the Vanderbilt University Divinity School.

A pulpit exchange with the Metropolitan Community Church started the interest in discussing homosexuality. Individual and congregational relationships were developed. This put faces on the social issue. The congregation also got involved with an HIV/AIDS ministry called CARES in Nashville. Educational programs on HIV/AIDS developed out of this. Gays and lesbians found their way into membership in the church. Conversation about starting an ONA study were met with the response, "We already are."

William Sloane Coffin Jr. admonished that Brookmeade Church was not really "open and affirming" until members declared it so. This challenge occurred around the same time as a congregation-wide survey was done. Some evidence surfaced about the discomfort of individuals with the presence of gays and lesbians in the congregation. These two factors together sparked the interest in an ONA study for the congregation.

The board of deacons provided leadership for the study. They sent for resources from the ONA program and set about to do the study itself first before making a proposal to the church council. The council received the proposal and asked the congregation for authority to move ahead. The plan, which was approved, included the following:

- At a potluck, members saw and discussed a video on becoming Open and Affirming.
- Two presentations and discussions on the Bible and theology were set up.
- A supper program with a gay pastor was held.
- A discussion session was planned with members of Parents, Families and Friends of Lesbians and Gays.
- An open session at which members could ask questions and express feelings concluded the process.

This last meeting was well led, and two counselors were present to help build trust and express feelings. A personal story told by a lesbian whose partner was also a member of the congregation came out of the open meeting and was shared in worship with the congregation one Sunday. This again personalized the issue.

Communication with the whole congregation was attempted through newsletter articles on the process. Personal contact was made with people who were not seen at the study or who were known to be opposed to the study. Ground rules for all sessions were employed for sharing in respect and love.

The decision-making session resulted in a declaration that the congregation was Open and Affirming. No members were lost as a result of the decision. In fact, the process evoked a closer and more honest community with a renewed sense of mission. The gay pastor provides leadership in the larger community for interfaith and social concerns.

Analysis

Based on what I believe to be the studies' relevant material, summarized above, I have several observations and some theoretical insights about the dynamics of these cases. Of course, my own readings and writing, along with my work with congregations in conflict, inform my perceptions. I hope the following will be helpful to those who have yet to try discussing homosexuality.

1. The degree to which an individual or group has come to know and to accept itself will greatly affect the way in which that person or group deals with conflict and change. The more accurate the self-knowledge and the higher the degree of self-acceptance, the less defensive and the more open that person or group will be to conflict and change. This principle applies to church members as well as to entire congregations.

Those congregations that had the most success with the study process had worked in advance on their sense of self-image and mission. They already saw themselves as inclusive and affirming of people outside their membership, viewing others as children of God who are loved and accepted by God. They did have to deal with their unconscious prejudices, but that proved to be growth enhancing. Establishing a vision and then attempting to live that vision proved to be critical dimensions of those congregations who were most successful with their experience. The church leaders, both clergy and lay, who continually held up the vision as the context for study, were also able to help those who questioned themselves to work out their inner conflict. With that skill leaders also assisted the congregation as a whole to deal with its internal conflict.

In those congregations that had to deal with individual antagonists, it appears that each antagonist had a personal life issue or issues with the congregation that had not been worked through. The result of that personal dynamic was the projection of that unresolved conflict on the present scene. Attempts to resolve the conflict were unsuccessful because the mediation was not dealing with the underlying issue(s). Unresolved conflict coming out of a study will surely affect future decision-making dynamics.

2. The congregations with the most successful studies were those with the highest degree of involvement or attempted involvement in the process. First Congregational Church, which had the least success, had the least degree of involvement in the study and subsequent move to make a congregational statement. When people feel left out and not heard, they will resist the study process. People's resistance does not depend on whether they agree with the position(s) being discussed. Those who disagree with an issue or proposed statement will tend to accept the statement, after stating their disagreement, and will go along with the majority *when* they feel they have been heard. If they do not feel heard, their initial antagonism will tend to prevail.

3. Another basic policy when dealing with group conflict is to use ground rules based on the community's self-concept. Having a vision and covenant helps in this regard. When a congregation has a clear statement of itself as a loving and accepting (inclusive) community, it can easily establish ground rules for discussion that lead to careful listening and acceptance of differences. Leaders of such discussions can readily refer to the ground rules when the interaction seems to be outside the set parameters. Having ground rules would have helped in some of the cases when individuals or groups seem to respond negatively to people instead of to their ideas—an important distinction to be maintained by the group leader.

4. To find common ground in conflict, it is essential that participants agree on the meaning of words and experiences. There is often a frustrating breakdown in group discussions because individuals are trying to find common ground over what seems to be an obvious point and they can find no agreement. Communication is often stymied when the assumption is made that the meaning of a critical word in a statement is held to be the same by all parties. The meaning of words varies according to the experience of the individual or group. In the case of First Congregational Church, the word *affirming* was a major stumbling block because it meant different things to different people. Perceptions about

what has happened in group experiences may also differ, and to the degree that interpretations of the experience differ, the community will not be able to build on the experience and move forward as a whole. Assumptions about the meaning of words and experiences are a major deterrent to working through conflict. Assumptions block progress and leave no apparent way to get beyond the blocks. Group leaders in particular need to be aware of this as they lead discussions.

5. The recognition of the difference between win/lose and win/win situations and group leaders' skill to move from win/lose to win/win seemed to play a role in our cases. Where visioning and covenanting were integral to the congregational process, it was easier to reach and work with a win/win mode than where that was not the case. Viewing ideas as "right" or "wrong" rather than simply "yours" or "mine" can lead to unresolvable debates. The competition divides rather than showing a creative diversity amidst the variance of God's whole, good creation. One of the learnings from the successful congregational cases was reported to be a realization that the community does not have to agree on all things in order to be loving and affirming. This realization affirmed the possibilities of win/win and the unnecessary destructive nature of win/lose.

6. The decisionmaking process itself is an important ingredient to dealing constructively with conflict. One of the churches in the case studies, Zion UCC, had made the decision to use a consensus style of decisionmaking throughout the church community. This process allows all persons to feel that he or she is important to every decision. No one is rolled over, as is possible when decisions are made on the basis of the majority's vote. Consensus-style decision making makes use of a win/win model, rather than a win/lose framework. Every majority vote experience sets up a polarity—some win and some lose. This in turn gives rise to feelings that the losers will likely carry over into the next issue and prohibits cleanly addressing each issue. For instance, as in the First Congregational case study, it is quite possible the decision about moving the church, the congregation's not calling the black minister, and the minority's feelings on the issues of women in ministry and inclusive language all influenced the debate on the ONA issue, so the homosexuality issue was actually a combination of issues that had not been clearly dealt with.

Consensus methodology is a process that requires great skill. Unfortunately, group leaders try to use it without preparation and become discouraged. Group leadership and facilitation take training. Learning consensus-style decision making requires additional work, which is very worthwhile.

7. The discussion and study of a social issue as an intellectual exercise is far different from the study of one that has faces and personal experience associated with it. The abstract and theoretical approach is often an enjoyable exercise for some, but it must be carefully monitored if there is an intent to bring an issue to the congregation for action. The case study from Edina Community Lutheran Church testified to the critical nature of a panel session with gay or lesbian members of the church and representatives of families who had gay or lesbian children or other relatives. This experience brought the discussion from "they" to "we" or "us." The "issue" became faces and people members knew, rather than a projected, theoretical group. This made all the difference for Edina. It also entered significantly into the case studies of Fresno, Brookmeade, and Dayton Avenue churches. It can make a major difference in all studies of social issues.

The major learning that seems to emerge from all of these cases is that it is worthwhile to engage in constructive conflict rather than exist in harmonious dishonesty. There are skills to be learned for dealing with conflict constructively, and these need to be a part of lay and pastoral leadership training for each congregation. The more experience a congregation has successfully addressing conflict, the better able members will be to create win/win scenarios even when dealing with topics as potentially divisive as homosexuality. The benefits of having dealt with any issue successfully and having come to know other members more deeply in the process builds and strengthens the community. More meaningful relationships develop among members, and an understanding emerges that the hard work makes a difference. We no longer view difficult issues as roadblocks to effective ministry. Rather, we are inspired by these issues to be self-aware and clear in our communication. We are reminded that we are called to be a broad and deep community and to love even those with whom we disagree. And we are encouraged to see not just issues but the people behind them.

CHAPTER 13

Comforting or Challenging the Congregation?

Speed Leas
Boulder Creek, California

In the foreword to this book, I discussed the reasons for and against a congregation's taking a stand on controversial issues. One of the major concerns is whether the congregation is ready for stress or in need of comfort at a given time in its life. Certainly congregations need both calm and challenge for healthy functioning. I have found that Barry Johnson's thinking on polarity management (*Polarity Management: Identifying and Managing Unsolvable Problems,* HRD Press, 1992) helps me to understand congregations' experience of both these positive organizational needs, as well as how to move between them. By way of introducing the general concept of polarity management, let's look at some of the characteristics of the calm/challenge polarity.

Polarities

This need to incorporate both comfort and challenge in the life of a congregation is a specific instance of what Johnson calls a polarity. According to authors Roy Oswald and Robert Friedrich, "a key principle of polarity theory states: Problems can be solved; conflicts can be resolved; but polarities can only be managed. Your only choice is whether you will manage them well or manage them poorly." They go on to explain that each "pole" of a polarity has both a positive and a negative side, and "the negative side of each pole is corrected by moving to the positive side of the opposite pole. In this way, the poles are interdependent, and there is no way out of the dilemma."[1] I will not attempt to explain Johnson's model fully, but readers who would like to learn more about this rich, deep concept are encouraged to explore his book. I do, however, want to make use of several key concepts from his work. In my opinion, the polarity between challenging and comforting is one of the key issues with regard to managing a healthy congregation. The various issues can be mapped as follows:

+	+
People need to be aware of the needs of others	People have many stresses in life, they need comfort
People should take care of their neighbors	Good work is a function of support, training, and development
It is one purpose of a church or synagogue to set high standards	Renewal is a function of rest
Churches should challenge their constituents	**Churches should comfort their constituents**
The self-righteousness that comes from doing good works is annoying to many	Comfort leads to self-centeredness
Workaholics burn out	Comfort leads to complacency
Challenge can mean you lose donors and some who don't like the issue being raised	Comfort is not responsive to others' needs
−	−

Interdependence, Not Balance

Challenging and comforting do not function separately from one another, even though in a way they are opposites. Each needs the other. A
stressed person needs comfort if he or she is burning out; a comfortable
person may well need stress if he or she is getting lazy and sloppy. But
we need to maintain a tension between the two functions in a healthy
organism. The relationship between challenge and comfort is like breath-
ing: We need to exhale *and* we need to inhale. It might be that some or
most healthy congregations spend a great deal more time on comfort
than they do challenge. The question here is, What does this congregation need at this time?

Flexibility

Another important dimension of a polarity is that movement is required.
A well-functioning polarity is one that is not stuck. Movement *should*
happen. We might think of a teeter-totter here. What makes a teeter-
totter fun is not balancing the weights on the ends of the board; it is the
up-and-down movement. As one person goes up, the other goes down.
As I give up on comfort, I take on challenge; as I give up challenge, I
enjoy comfort. Each is good, and each requires that I let go, to a significant degree, of the other. Individuals and groups tend to move among
the various aspects of a polarity as follows:

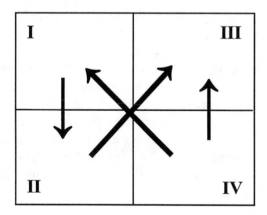

Without movement, it is likely that the organism will experience both the positive and negative aspects (upside and downside) of only one pole (such as comfort) and not the benefit of the other pole (in this case, challenge). It does not matter on which side of the polarity the system is stuck. Problems arise on either end if the system is no longer moving. The polarity is well managed when we prevent the system from either becoming stuck or going far into the downside of each pole.

When a system has been focusing for too long on comfort, it will manifest the following symptoms:

- Members fear challenge.
- Members do not show up at meetings to discuss controversial issues.
- The system is characterized by loss of energy and lethargy.
- People are squelched if they raise questions or attempt to hold opinions different from those assumed to be held by the majority.

What is called for at this time is not greater doses of comfort but a risk, a leap of faith, a challenge to the system. What will help the system to take risks is hearing that others have risked and lived, learning ways to deal with the questions and tensions that will arise, having a plan to move ahead toward a decision or a learning goal, and the knowledge that the system will be moving back to the upside of the comfort pole after having done well on the challenge.

When is it time to move back to the comfort pole?

- Members are getting burned out.
- The congregation is becoming a one-issue church or synagogue.
- The positions people take are hard and unreasonable, and there is no room for dissent from what is "politically correct."

One way to help a congregation respond to its stuckness or movement far into the downside of one pole is to have a regular cycle of challenge and bringing comfort, actually to schedule shifts in the organization's attention. Commonly congregations shift their attention from planning to doing. The board goes on retreat once a year to plan and the rest of the year works from the plans established at the retreat. There is no reason a congregation could not manage the comfort/challenge polarity in such a manner, if it chooses to.

Simultaneity

I doubt it is possible for one part of a system to address two poles of any given polarity at the same time. But it should be possible for both poles to be addressed by different parts of the system. For example, a congregation might have at the same time both a prayer group for the bereaved and a social action group for those who want to challenge issues in the community. It is probably not possible, however, for the prayer group to challenge at the same time it is providing comfort, or for the social action group to provide comfort at the same moment it is challenging.

Leadership

Examining where a congregation stands with regard to comfort and challenge is important for congregations exploring the possibility of talking about homosexuality. The skill and readiness of the congregation's leaders, which are key to successfully seeing a congregation through a challenge, must also be assessed. Following the lead of Edwin Friedman (*Generation to Generation: Family Process in Church and Synagogue,* Guilford Press, 1985) and others, I believe change (which always presents challenges) that is intentional is change that is led. Change, of course, sometimes comes about because of demographic, evolutionary, or developmental factors beyond the control of an organization or the people in it. But change also happens because someone planned it. New buildings, new worship patterns, new programs come from planned change. But what is needed to lead change?

1. A leader has been granted authority by the congregation.

In a congregation, some functions of headship are not automatically given to the person who happens to be the rabbi or pastor. The congregation must first make a commitment to this clergyperson. Members will ask, in effect, Can he or she be trusted? Should we let him or her lead? As the system discovers that the pastor or rabbi is trustworthy, it grants more authority to the person. Note, however, that headship is rarely, if ever, given completely. The congregation or members always reserve the right to withhold or take back certain dimensions of headship—or all of it. For example, the congregation might give the pastor the right to make decisions about staff but not about changing worship, or the right to tell them what their denomination believes but not the right to tell them what they personally should believe.

This headship is not given all at once. It is given slowly and in dollops. It takes time for a pastor to be fully enough enrolled in the system as leader that the congregation will give her or him permission to lead on issues that threaten the system. The longer a pastor is in the system, the more she or he accrues authority to lead. Therefore, it is not a good idea for a new pastor or rabbi to address a threatening issue.

Leadership, however, is not merely a function of longevity. Before a leader is given authority in the system, she or he will have demonstrated to the congregation (1) respect and appreciation for its traditions, goals, and values; (2) competence to deal with challenges; (3) ability to comfort and challenge the congregation, so members will know the clergyperson will not leave them stuck or on the downside of a polarity.

Leadership does not happen until the congregation has enrolled the pastor in this position *and* members have enrolled themselves in complementary follower roles. By "follower," I mean that members are open to listening, exploring ideas and suggestions, and joining with the leader in cooperative efforts to change, rather than resisting all initiatives the leader makes.

2. A leader has a map.

Leadership is not leadership unless it challenges the current situation. This principle is the very core of what leadership means. When an organization is in chaos, when the system is under siege, a leader helps the system move out of the current upset into stability. When the system is stable and homeostatic forces seem to predominate, a leader brings about appropriate change within the system. If a leader is going to lead, she or he must have an idea about where the organization can go, what it can do, how it should respond. Without a vision of how the organization can be different and without sharing that vision, the congregation stays stuck. It is not led.

John Kotter, author of *Leading Change* (Harvard Business School

Press, 1996), believes that for a leader to lead, his or her values must to a very large degree match those of the people in the system, and the people within the system must perceive that fact. If the leader's values and those of the congregation do not overlap significantly, the members are not likely to pay attention or continue to grant the leader headship. This does not mean the values are the same, however. If the leader's values and those of the congregation are identical, the tension required for change will not be present in the system. Tension must exist for there to be energy or impetus for change. One can see from the cases in this book that the map provided by a leader must include:

- Clear goals. Are we going to study the issue? Are we going to take a public stand? Are we going to change our bylaws or our operating procedures because of this decision? Are we going to change the way we induct new members into the congregation or the way we train ushers and greeters, for example?
- Clear values. The leader is not closed to others' points of view, but he or she has wrestled with the values questions and is able to articulate well and clearly a perspective that the leader believes is good and useful and should be adopted by the congregation.
- Clear process. Leaders offer ideas about procedure as well as about goals and values. The system is more likely to change if its members are helped to explore *how* it will change as well as *what* changes are intended. Even though a leader has an idea about how the congregation will proceed, however, the leader can be open to and responsive to others' ideas.

3. A leader chooses to generate some anxiety in the system.

The role of the leader is neither to provoke anxiety nor to make it go away. It is to work with the anxiety present in the system. Yes, people are anxious, especially about controversy and particularly about sexual behavior. But when the leader focuses on the anxiety, she or he misses the point. The point has to do with whether the system needs to change, how much it needs to change, and whether it will change—not whether it will have anxiety. So the leader can confirm what it happening in the system: "Yes, we are experiencing tension, but we are managing it well."

Or perhaps, "Yes, we are experiencing tension, and the way we are man-aging it can be improved; here are some ideas about how to manage the tension (but not make it go away)."

The leader will be greatly helped by being rooted not only in the system he or she is trying to change but also in other systems that will help him or her keep a perspective on the anxiety of the system he or she is trying to change. Leaders who can say (to themselves or aloud), "I've been in other situations like this and survived," or "I know of others who have taken on such changes as this, and they have survived, and the sys-tem survived," have a much better chance of monitoring and regulating anxiety than those who have no other reference.

4. A leader's anxiety is visible but managed.

On occasion Friedman's description of the leader as a nonanxious pre-sence is misinterpreted to mean leaders should be totally nonanxious. I believe Friedman's point is not that a leader is zombie-like but that the leader is recognized as real, as a part of what is going on. When some-one tries to function in a way that says, "Worry? Not me!" the people say to themselves, "This person doesn't get it. This person has no fear, and I am concerned that she or he may not be concerned for our safety." The pilot who says over the intercom, "We are about to enter rough weather, but I am first concerned about our safety, and I know how to handle this situation, so I will not put you into unnecessary danger," en-genders more confidence than the pilot who says, "Storms don't scare me! I've never seen a storm I didn't like! A good storm cleans out the weak and the sickly."

5. A leader stays connected.

Friedman says a leader is nonanxious *and* stays connected. Leaders know, respect, care for, empathize with, and encourage their followers. Leaders promote togetherness; they are not aloof and distant. When members participate in a discussion about whether the congregation will declare itself open to gays and lesbians, they have to have some evi-dence that although they are struggling with an issue that may separate them, they are also in a relationship that is as important as the dispute.

A leader must acknowledge that she or he is different from some members of the congregation (that is, has slightly different values, goals, perspectives) but at the same time must say, "I want to stay in relationship; I want to stay connected; we have much to gain and to learn from one another." Most leaders will be able to live with the tension of disagreeing while staying connected, although this is always difficult to do.

Assessing a Congregation

Based on our discussion, then, of the comfort/challenge polarity and of the leadership issues related to congregational life, the following questions need to be addressed when assessing a congregation's readiness to talk about homosexuality or other difficult issues.

1. How long has the pastor or rabbi been with the congregation?

Moving on an issue too soon, especially if the leader takes a side, is likely to threaten the clergyperson's continued leadership in the congregation. The system must be confident the leader is "one of us" before it will accept a challenge from him or her. How long must the leader wait? I do not believe one answer fits all, but the clergyperson certainly must wait longer than a year, and more likely three to five years, before the congregation will be ready to accept his or her leadership regarding a challenge to the congregation.

Could a congregation take on a difficult question *before* the pastor has been enrolled as leader? I think the answer is a qualified yes: It would be possible if there is a group (or individual) in the congregation that has been enrolled as leader. The clergyperson, however, would not play the role of leader in such a case. He or she would more likely act as consultant or mediator, helping all sides function in ways that are fair and keep the system together, focusing more on the "staying connected" part of the Friedman polarity than on the self-differentiated part. By and large, however, most congregations do not have enough clarity or agreement about who the enrolled lay leaders are for the congregation to take on a challenge before a rabbi or pastor has been enrolled as leader.

2. Does the rabbi or pastor have the skills to provide leadership through a difficult dialogue?

The first question was, Will the congregation give the clergy the right to lead? This question is, *Can* the clergy lead? I believe leadership, like tennis, is a skill that can be taught, but not everyone can be a good tennis player—or leader. How well a person might lead is sometimes difficult to assess, especially if the clergyperson desperately wants to be a leader but does not seem to be able to pull it off. I recommend that before a pastor or rabbi takes on a difficult issue like homosexuality, she or he needs to have a track record of leadership in other arenas.

3. Is the rabbi or pastor able to withstand the heat generated by the anxiety that will certainly arise in the congregation?

This issue needs the serious attention of those assessing a leader's readiness to take on a difficult task. It is entirely possible the clergyperson has successfully provided leadership in the past but at this point is particularly vulnerable to the anxiety of others in this system. Readiness in this arena should be assessed not only through the clergy's self-analysis but by those close to the leader who might also be able to help assess his or her tolerance for stress at this time.

4. Can the key leaders in the congregation take the heat?

Not only must the clergy leader be able to take it, but the congregation must be ready for the issue. It might be that a given congregation will take years to get ready to address a difficult issue. I believe some congregations will never be able to discuss homosexuality because (1) the tension would be too great; (2) the members are too vulnerable; (3) the system does not have norms (tacit rules) for managing conflict in healthy ways; or (4) the congregation has not successfully dealt with other difficult issues in the past. All of these would be good reasons to work through a less explosive issue before tackling homosexuality.

5. Is the congregation currently dealing with other stressful issues?

A congregation should make an effort not to fight a two- or three-front war. Decisions about whether this or that staff member should stay, whether to erect a new building, or whether to bring in a new religious education curriculum should not be settled at the same time a value-laden issue such as homosexuality is addressed. A favorite strategy of those trying to derail a good learning process is to distract people's attention from the main issue and to "complexify" the situation to such a degree that no one can meaningfully focus on the issue at hand.

Overall Advice

Here are some hints for leaders of congregations that want to address difficult issues such as homosexuality:

1. Ask for the congregation's advice.

When members of a congregation feel excluded, they are likely to rebel, repudiate, or resist. To minimize these reactions, include members appropriately in the decisionmaking. The more members are able to facilitate the congregation's participation in the decisionmaking, including shaping the process and the questions to be addressed, the less inappropriate resistance there will be to the discussion or decisions. In some situations, the congregation cannot make a certain decision, or the decision is made by the leaders or the larger denomination, but asking for advice and guidance from people before taking action will likely have a positive impact on the decisionmaking.

2. Demonstrate that you value others' views.

Even though you might not agree with the views of some in the congregation, the more you are able to show respect for at least a part of what is shaping another person's position (even if you cannot agree with all the reasoning or conclusions the other makes), the more likely the other will function in appropriate ways. The way each party in a dispute about values approaches the other will affect how the other responds. The temptation is to respond to anger with anger, hyperbole with hyperbole. Conflict de-escalates (among healthy people) when one party is able to respond in ways other than those established by the other party. Instead of responding to anger with anger, respond to anger by establishing boundaries. Instead of responding to hyperbole with extravagance, respond to it with tempered reason, inviting the other to do the same.

3. Organize forums to search for God's will rather than to debate.

In some settings it might be more meaningful to use language such as, "Let us search for what binds us in the faith" or "...search for the good of the whole" or "...seek to find areas of agreement" or "...identify our values in this situation." People engaged in conflict management know that although debate is interesting in the classroom, it is not helpful when groups seek to take responsible action. By "debate," I mean a process focused exclusively on differentiating one side from another rather than searching for shared truth or meaning. There is a place for challenging ideas and values and meanings. The value of the challenge, however, is lost if the challenge is not held in tension with a commitment to finding greater truth or common commitment.

4. Take your time; don't rush.

Rushing generates anxiety. Rushing leads some people to believe there is something to hide, a reason not to explore these important issues in depth. When dealing with an issue that for some people is strange or deviates from the ordinary, the strangeness is a significant part of the problem. Helping members become used to talking about these issues and familiar with their complexity will help them learn more and make better decisions by bringing more of their intellectual, emotional, and spiritual resources to the task.

Familiarity with the issue of homosexuality does not necessarily mean people are going to agree to become more open and affirming of homosexuals. But their resistance will be based less on "I don't like anything that is different from what I understand or am familiar with" and more on "I have come to this conclusion based on thoughtful exploration, prayer, and exposure to people who know something about this issue in depth, even people I don't like, agree with, or completely understand."

5. Encourage people to talk about feelings.

Feelings influence decisions. They are a part of what shapes our thinking. Whether the feelings are aversive or attractive, becoming familiar with feelings and encouraging their appropriate expression will lead to fuller understanding and discussion.

Strategies for Talking about Homosexuality in a Congregation

The issue of homosexuality can be engaged on at least four levels.

1. Do nothing.

I really would not call this engagement, but it is the place from which a congregation might begin when moving from comfort toward challenge.

2. Preach about it.

If a clergyperson is going to preach about this subject, he or she is not as likely to impact long-held views on the subject as if the preaching is coupled with other opportunities for study and discussion. When the pastor has been enrolled as the tacit leader, however, preaching as part of an overall strategy makes use of a powerful leadership role.

3. Study the issue individually or in groups.

Many study methods can be used in a congregation. Each method will have a different impact, depending on members' reading and discussion skills and their willingness to join in a discernment process.

- Invite people interested in the subject to hear a lecture on the issue in a forum held between services or after or before a service.
- Invite people interested in the subject to study the issue in a group where different perspectives are presented by a speaker or through the use of videos and movies.
- Invite people interested in the subject to read about it individually.
- Invite people interested in the subject to read about the subject and then discuss it in small groups.
- Invite people interested in the subject to hear from those who have been affected by the issue: homosexuals or parents, siblings, children, or friends of homosexuals.

The above strategies will take the congregation to yet another level of engagement when participants include *all members,* not simply those who are interested in the topic.

4. Make a decision.

So far the study strategies all assume that the congregation itself will not take a position on the matter. Study is good, it will provide people with information, and in the long run, for most people, it will reduce anxiety about the subject. Study without some kind of commitment, however, will have far less impact on the policies (especially the tacit policies) of the congregation. Study without a decision on the part of the congregation will also make it easier for outsiders (and some insiders) to make assumptions about the congregation that might not be true. Using the study process to make a decision will increase the motivation of members to study carefully and to participate in a discussion they might otherwise ignore.

Conclusion

What you have seen in this book is a chronicle of congregations that
have taken on a difficult and important subject, thus providing an opportunity to push to the heart of religious experience and practice. Christians
would say the discussion "gives the church a chance to be the church"—
to take one another very seriously. Old and new ideas are challenged.
Those who are frightened or worn out are given courage and comfort.
Those who are ready are challenged. This issue is not the only one that
gives the church a chance to be the church, but it is an issue whose time
has come. Many congregations are ready. They need only take advantage of the resources available to give them the courage to take another
step.

NOTES

Preface

1. William C. McFadden, S.J., "Homosexuality," *The Modern Catholic Encyclopedia*, edited by Michael Glazier and Monika K. Hellwig (Collegeville, Minn.: The Liturgical Press, 1994), 400.

2. The United Church of Christ Fifteenth General Synod resolution, "Calling on United Church of Christ Congregations to Covenant as Open and Affirming," passed on July 2, 1985, by 95 percent of voting delegates.

3. Ronald A. Heifetz, *Leadership Without Easy Answers* (Cambridge, Mass.: The Belknap Press, 1994), 271.

Chapter 1: Talking about Sexuality

1. Marvin M. Ellison, *Erotic Justice* (Louisville, Ky.: Westminster John Knox Press, 1996), 1-2.

2. James B. Nelson, *Body Theology* (Louisville, Ky.: Westminster John Knox Press, 1992), 29.

3. From "Spirit Prayers: Prayers for More Light 1993," edited by Chris Glaser, *More Light Update* 13, no. 6 (January 1993): 5.

Chapter 2: Why Is Homosexuality So Hard to Talk About?

1. Will Campbell, "What's Religion Got to Do with Sex?" Questions of Faith Series, vol. 3 (Nashville: Ecufilm), 1990.

2. Bishop Leontine T. C. Kelly, "What's Religion Got to Do with Sex?"

3. Warren J. Blumenfeld, ed., *Homophobia: How We All Pay the Price* (Boston: Beacon Press, 1992), 5.

4. Vivienne C. Cass, "Homosexual Identity Formation: A Theoretical Model," *Journal of Homosexuality* 4, no. 3 (Spring 1979): 219-35.

5. Peter L. Steinke, *Healthy Congregations: A Systems Approach* (Bethesda, Md.: the Alban Institute, 1996), 4.

6. Cass, "Homosexual Identity Formation," 223.

7. Ibid.

8. William Sloane Coffin Jr., "What's Religion Got to Do with Sex?" Questions of Faith Series, vol. 3 (Nashville: Ecufilm), 1990.

9. Two organizations that assist gay men, lesbians, bisexual, and transgendered people and their families are:

Parents, Families and Friends of Lesbians and Gays (PFLAG)
1101 14th Street N.W., Suite 1030
Washington, D.C. 20005
202-638-4200

Children of Lesbians and Gays Everywhere (COLAGE)
2300 Market Street
Box 165
San Francisco, CA 94114
415-861-KIDS

10. A Reconciling Congregation is a United Methodist congregation that has publically affirmed that it welcomes gays, lesbians, and bisexuals.

11. A multidenominational resource is *Open Hands: Resources for Ministries Affirming the Diversity of Human Sexuality*. See the resources section for more information.

Chapter 3: Explosive Issues Require Special Handling

1. Speed Leas, *Moving Your Church Through Conflict* (Washington, D.C.: the Alban Institute, 1985).

2. Peter Senge, *The Fifth Discipline: The Art and Practice of the Learning Organization* (New York: Doubleday, 1990), 238-49.

Chapter 4: Rules for Talking about a Difficult Issue

1. Richard A. McCormick, S.J., "Rules for the Abortion Debate," in *Abortion: The Moral Issues*, edited by Edward Batchelor Jr. (New York: Pilgrim, 1982), 27-37; originally published in *America* (July 22, 1978).

2. See, for example, Marc Kolden, *Living the Faith*, Rejoice Sunday School Curriculum (Minneapolis: Augsburg Fortress, 1992), esp. chaps. 1, 3, 11, and 12. In addition to the work mentioned in note 1, see also Robert Benne, *Ordinary Saints* (Philadelphia: Fortress Press, 1988); Lewis Smedes, *Mere Morality* (Grand Rapids, Mich.: Wm. B. Eerdmans Publishing Co., 1983); and Jacques Thiroux, *Ethics: Theory and Practice*, 4th ed. (New York: Macmillan, 1990). The book by Thiroux is not written from a religious perspective but is a very useful tool for putting together arguments, understanding models, and using case studies. What implicit theology he has is very inadequate, but pastors and other leaders can rectify that when drawing on his many helpful ways of presenting materials.

Chapter 6: Dayton Avenue Presbyterian Church

1. Congregations of the Presbyterian Church (U.S.A.) that publicly welcome gays, lesbians, and bisexuals have formed the More Light Churches Network.

Chapter 8: Trinity United Methodist Church

1. "A Call for Renewal of Theology and Mission in the United Methodist Church: A Response to 'The Confessing Movement'" (Atlanta: Trinity United Methodist Church, 1995).
2. Ibid.
3. Ibid.
4. Dorothy Williams, "The Church Studies Homosexuality,"

Nashville: The United Methodist Publishing House, 1992. This study was comissioned by the General Conference of the United Methodist Church.

Chapter 10: Edina Community Lutheran Church

1. Reconciled in Christ congregations have publicly declared they welcome gays, lesbians, and bisexuals.

2. See the resource list at the end of this book for matierals to help congregations explore pertinent biblical passages.

Chapter 13: Comforting or Challenging the Congregation

1. Roy M. Oswald and Robert E. Friedrich, Jr., *Discerning Your Congregation's Future: A Strategic and Spiritual Approach* (Bethesda, Md.: The Alban Institute, 1996), 32.

RESOURCES

Books and Studies

Alexander, Marilyn Bennett, and James Preston. *We Were Baptized Too: Claiming God's Grace for Lesbians and Gays.* New York: Houghton Mifflin, 1992.
Challenges the church to take seriously its understanding of baptism and communion as a means of grace, justice, and liberation.

Avery, Michel, et al. *Building United Judgment: A Handbook for Consensus Decision Making.* Madison, Wis.: Center for Conflict Resolution, 1981.
Techniques and skills for effective consensus.

Brash, Alan A. *Facing Our Differences: The Churches and Their Gay and Lesbian Members.* Geneva: World Council of Churches Publications, 1995.
A look at issues of homosexuality in light of the theology and biblical interpretation of different church bodies around the world.

Brawley, Robert L., ed. *Biblical Ethics and Homosexuality: Listening to Scripture.* Louisville, Ky.: Westminster John Knox Press, 1996.
Twenty-four Bible scholars demonstrate the multiplicity of voices engaged in biblically responsible and constructive debates about sexuality.

Cleaver, Richard. *Know My Name: A Gay Liberation Theology.* Louisville, Ky.: Westminster John Knox Press, 1995.
Examines the struggles of gay men and lesbians in the church through

the lens of liberation theology. Offers a "gay reading" of Scripture that is spiritually challenging to all.

Cohen, Susan, and Daniel Cohen. *When Someone You Know Is Gay.* New York: M. Evans & Co., 1989.
Short, readable chapters. Written for young adults but good for adults too. Explores Scripture and theology.

Congregational Ministries Division, Presbyterian Church (U.S.A.). *Reconciling the Broken Silence: The Church in Dialogue on Gay and Lesbian Issues.* Louisville, Ky.: Presbyterian Church (U.S.A.), 1993.
Six-session study guide for congregations preparing to engage in honest and open dialogue with gay men and lesbians at a table that does not condemn them.

Cosgrove, Charles H., and Dennis D. Hatfield. *Church Conflict: The Hidden Systems Behind the Fights.* Nashville: Abingdon, 1994.
Uses an analogy between the church and the family to show how family-like rules operate within churches.

Geis, Sally B., and Donald E. Messer, eds. *Caught in the Crossfire: Helping Christians Debate Homosexuality.* Nashville: Abingdon, 1994.
Offers a range of views on issues such as biblical interpretation, science, ordination, gay unions. Includes discussion questions for group use.

Griffin, Carolyn Welch, Marian J. Wirth, and Arthur G. Wirth. *Beyond Acceptance: Parents of Lesbians and Gays Talk about Their Experiences.* New York: St. Martin's Press Inc., 1990.
Excellent resource describing experiences of parents of lesbians and gays, with well-researched answers to often-asked questions.

Halverstadt, Hugh F. *Managing Church Conflict.* Louisville, Ky.: Westminster John Knox Press, 1991.
Draws on organizational group process to examine theological and ethical issues surrounding conflict. Advocates a focus on the common good.

Helminiak, Daniel A. *What the Bible Really Says about Homosexuality:*

Recent Findings by Top Scholars Offer a Radical New View. San
Francisco: Alamo Square Press, 1994.
A thoughtful, lucid, and accessible summary of current biblical scholar-
ship.

Hilton, Bruce. *Can Homophobia Be Cured?* Nashville: Abingdon,
1992.
Written by a Methodist, the director of the National Center for Bioeth-
ics. Each chapter addresses a question, such as, What do we know about
gay people? What does the Bible say? What does the church say?

Leas, Speed. *Leadership and Conflict.* Nashville: Abingdon Press,
1982.
A standard in the field.

Long, Patricia V. *Enlarging the Circle: Pullen's Holy Union Process.*
Raleigh, N.C.: Pullen Memorial Baptist Church, 1996.
The story of Pullen Memorial Baptist Church's ministry to gay men
and lesbians. Available from Pullen Memorial Baptist Church, 1801
Hillsborough Street, Raleigh, NC 27605.

Mollenkott, Virginia Ramey, and Letha Scanzoni. *Is the Homosexual
My Neighbor? Another Christian View.* San Francisco: Harper and
Row, 1978.
Two respected evangelical Christians consider Scripture and other mat-
ters related to homosexuality.

O'Neill, Craig, and Kathleen Ritter. *Coming Out Within: Stages of
Spiritual Awakening for Lesbians and Gay Men.* San Francisco:
HarperSanFrancisco, 1992.
Describes an eight-stage process by which poignant loss can facilitate
personal and spiritual transformation.

Osterman, Mary Jo. *Claiming the Promise: An Ecumenical Welcoming
Bible Study Resource on Homosexuality.* Chicago: Reconciling Con-
gregations Program, 1996.
Well-researched, highly accessible, seven-session study written in con-
sultation with biblical scholars from several Christian denominations.
Separate leader's guide.

Pronk, Pim. *Against Nature? Types of Moral Argumentation Regarding Homosexuality*. Grand Rapids, Mich.: Wm. B. Eerdmans Publishing Co., 1993.
Reexamines the church's attitude toward ethics in general and homosexuality in particular.

Scroggs, Robin. *The New Testament and Homosexuality: Contextual Background for Contemporary Debate*. Philadelphia: Fortress Press, 1983.
Easy-to-read review of Greek, Palestinian Jewish, and Hellenistic Jewish cultures and related study of Pauline usage of the Greek language.

Seifert, Harvey, and Lois Seifert. *When Christians Disagree*. Brea, Calif.: Educational Ministries, 1991.
Eight-session adult study on conflicts and decision making related to world peace, economic justice, abortion, political freedom, homosexuality, and preserving the earth.

Seow, Choon-Leong, ed. *Homosexuality and Christian Community*. Louisville, Ky.: Westminster John Knox, 1996.
Members of the Princeton Theological Seminary faculty address exegetical, interpretive, and practical issues pertaining to homosexuality.

Siker, Jeffrey S. *Homosexuality in the Church: Both Sides of the Debate*. Louisville, Ky.: Westminster John Knox, 1994.
Topics covered include Scripture, Christian tradition, moral reasoning, and decisionmaking.

Thorson-Smith, Sylvia. *Reconciling the Broken Silence: The Church in Dialogue on Gay and Lesbian Issues*. Louisville, Ky.: Congregational Ministries Division, Presbyterian Church (U.S.A.), 1993.
Six-session study provides language and opportunity for dialogue. First two sessions particularly address Presbyterian issues.

Periodicals

Concord: Newsletter of Lutherans Concerned/North America
Subscriptions are included with membership in LC/NA or are available
separately for $20.00/year for nonmembers. The membership lists of
LC/NA and *Concord* are strictly confidential. P.O. Box 10461 First
Dearborn Station, Chicago, IL 60610-0461.

More Light Update
Monthly magazine published by Presbyterians for Lesbian and Gay
Concerns. PLGC, P.O. Box 98, New Brunswick, NJ 08903. 908-249-
1016. Also see *More Light Churches Network Newsletter*. Published
periodically for congregations and individuals committed to this ministry. 360 West 55th Street, Apt. 6L, New York, NY 10019. 212-765-
1797.

*Open Hands: Resources for Ministries Affirming the Diversity of
Human Sexuality*
Published quarterly, this magazine is for congregations and individuals
seeking to be in ministry with gay, lesbian, and bisexual people. Each
issue focuses on a specific area of concern within the church. It is published by the Reconciling Congregation Program, Inc. (United Methodist), in cooperation with the Association of Welcoming and Affirming
Baptists (American Baptist), the More Light Churches Network (Presbyterian Church [U.S.A.]), Open and Affirming (United Church of Christ),
and Reconciled in Christ (Evangelical Lutheran Church in America)
programs. Reconciling Congregation Program, 3801 North Keeler
Avenue, Chicago, IL 60641. 773-736-5526.

Second Stone
A national, ecumenical gay and lesbian Christian news journal. Published
six times a year. Second Stone, P.O. Box 8340, New Orleans, LA
70182.

Waves
The national newsletter of the United Church Coalition for Lesbian/Gay
Concerns. Published quarterly. Confidential mailing list. UCCL/GC,
P.O. Box 403, Holden, MA 01520-0403.

Videos and Audiotapes

A Journey of Faith
Documents the experience of three UCC churches in southern California
as they explore declaring themselves Open and Affirming. Comes with
ONA background information and worship resources. 55 minutes. ONA
Video Resources, UCBHM-DAMA, 700 Prospect Avenue, Cleveland,
OH 44115-1100.

Always My Kid: A Family Guide to Understanding Homosexuality
Explores personal stories of coming out and the reactions and questions
that immediately follow. 74 minutes. From Triangle Video Productions,
550 Westcott, Suite 400, Houston, TX. 77007. 713-869-4477.

An Unexpected Journey: Parents and Friends of Lesbians and Gays
Shows families dealing with loved ones' coming out, and the pain of
lesbians, gay men, and their family members, as well as the joy of reconciliation. 29 minutes. PFLAG-Denver, P.O. Box 18901, Denver, CO
80218. 303-333-0286.

Can We Just Talk about It? The Church and Homosexuality
Ben Johnson, professor of Christian spirituality at Columbia Theological
Seminary, interviews a candidate for the ordained ministry; Dr. Walter
Brueggemann, professor of Old Testament; and Dr. Charles Cousar,
professor of New Testament, both of the seminary. 35 minutes. CTS
Press, 701 Columbia Drive, Decatur, GA 30031. 404-289-8952.

Can We Talk About This?
Highly recommended audiotape and six-session study guide for Chris-
tians preparing to discuss homosexuality. Produced by the Evangelical
Lutheran Church in America. Available from ELCA Distribution Center,
P.O. 1209, 100 South Fifth Street, Minneapolis, MN 55440-1209. 800-
328-4648.

Conflict in the Church: Division or Diversity?
Focuses on different styles of handling congregational conflict. Includes
study guide. 12 minutes. Mennonite Central Committee. P.O. Box 500,
Akron, PA 17501. 717-859-3889.

Life Stories on Growing Up Gay in the Christian Church
Stories of six gay or lesbian Christians. Has been broadcast by numerous California cable television stations. 48 minutes, ideal for two 24-minute presentations,. The Lazarus Project, 7350 Sunset Boulevard, West Hollywood, CA 90046.

Straight from the Heart
Moving account of parents' struggle upon learning their child is lesbian or gay. 24 minutes. Straight from the Heart, Woman Vision, 3145 Geary Boulevard, Box 421, San Francisco, CA 94118.

This Is My Story
Designed for people who are going through a personal struggle to reconcile their faith and their sexual orientation. InfoX, P.O. Box 67114, Cuyahoga Falls, OH 44222.

What's Religion Got to Do with Sex? Questions of Faith III
Addresses the Judeo-Christian perspective on sexuality, ministry to non-traditional relationships, and responses to homosexuality. Study guide available. 27 minutes. EcuFilm, 810 Twelfth Avenue South, Nashville, TN 37203. 800-251-4091; 615-242-6277 (TN).

Organizations

Because organizations tend to have a steady turnover in leadership, addresses and phone numbers for some of the following groups might change over time.

Affirming Congregation Program (ACP)
United Church of Canada
3150 Bloor Square West
Etobicoke, Ontario
Canada M8X 2Y4
416-231-7680, ext. 4141
Welcoming congregations of the United Church of Canada.

Children of Lesbians and Gays Everywhere (COLAGE)
2300 Market St.
Box 165
San Francisco, CA 94114
415-861-KIDS
An organization for people who have a gay or lesbian parent.

The More Light Churches Network (MLCN)
5525 Timber Lane
Excelsior, MN 55331
612-470-0093
Inclusive Presbyterian congregations. A reproducible, seven-page list of resources is available from Ralph Carter, 111 Milburn Street, Rochester, NY 14607-2918. 716-271-7649.

Oasis
21 Rector Street
Newark, NJ 07102
201-621-8151
Welcoming congregations of the Episcopal Church.

Open and Affirming Ministries (O&A)
1010 Park Avenue
New York, NY 10028-0991
212-288-3246
Inclusive Christian Church (Disciples of Christ) congregations.

Open and Affirming Program (ONA)
P.O. Box 403
Holden, MA. 01520
508-856-9316
Churches in the United Church of Christ that welcome gays, lesbians, and bisexual people.

Parents, Families and Friends of Lesbians and Gays (PFLAG)
1101 14th Street N.W., Suite 1030
Washington, DC 20005
202-638-4200

Promotes the health and well-being of gays, lesbian, and bisexual people and their families and friends. A number of publications are available, most for under $5.00 per copy. Call or write for a list.

Reconciled in Christ Program (RIC)
P.O. Box 10461
Fort Dearborn Station
Chicago, IL 60610
404-266-9615
Evangelical Lutheran Church in America congregations that welcome gays, lesbians, and bisexuals.

Reconciling Congregation Program, Inc. (RCP)
3801 North Keeler Avenue
Chicago, IL 60641
312-736-5526
An organization of inclusive United Methodist congregations.

Supportive Congregations Network (SCN)
P.O. Box 6300
Minneapolis, MN 55406
612-722-6906
Brethren/Mennonite congregations that are welcoming to homosexuals.

Welcoming and Affirming Baptists
P.O. Box 2596
Attleboro Falls, MA 02763
508-226-1945
Inclusive American Baptist congregations.

Welcoming Congregations Program (WCP)
25 Beacon Street
Boston, MA 03208
Inclusive Unitarian Universalist Association congregations.

Acknowledgments

This list was compiled with the assistance of Janelle Bussert, assistant professor of religion, Augsburg College, Minneapolis, Minnesota; Ralph Carter, Rochester, New York, who prepares lists of resources for The More Light Churches Network; and Ann B. Day, Holden, Massachusetts, coordinator of the Open and Affirming Program. These people also provided valuable background information and other assistance throughout this project.

CONTRIBUTORS

Frank Baldwin is senior pastor of First Congregational Church (United Church of Christ) in Fresno, California. He has been married to Margaret Lovejoy Baldwin for 30 years and is the father of three grown children.

Donald E. Bossart is retired from teaching at The Iliff School of Theology, where he specialized in courses on conflict resolution and interpersonal ministries. He is an ordained United Methodist minister.

Shirlee M. Bromley is pastor of Mira Vista United Church of Christ in El Cerrito, California. She has a D.Min. from Hartford Seminary and before entering seminary was a missionary in the Philippine Islands.

Carl S. Dudley is codirector of the Center for Social and Religious Research and professor of church and community at Hartford Seminary. He is author and coauthor of numerous books, including *Studying Congregations* (Abingdon, 1998) and *Next Steps toward Community Ministry* (Alban, 1996), and has been a pastor in metropolitan and cross-cultural congregations.

J. Bennett Guess is pastor and teacher at Zion United Church of Christ in Henderson, Kentucky. He is a graduate of Vanderbilt University Divinity School.

Hugh F. Halverstadt is professor of ministry, McCormick Theological Seminary, consultant to conflicted churches, trainer in middle judicatories, and author of *Managing Church Conflict* (Westminister John

Knox, 1991). An ordained Presbyterian, he has served as head of staff, solo pastor, interim minister, and in new church development.

Pamela Johnson has been a member of Edina Commuity Lutheran Church since 1984, where she has served in various leadership positions. She often speaks at forums in other congregations that are considering becoming Reconciled in Christ.

Marc Kolden is academic dean and professor of systematic theology at Luther Seminary, Saint Paul, Minnesota. Previously he served as a pastor at Our Redeemer's Lutheran Church, Helena, Montana.

Speed Leas is a senior consultant with the Alban Institute. He has written several books on the subject of conflict and churches, including *Discover Your Conflict Management Style* (Rev. Ed, Alban, 1997).

Karen A. McClintock is minister of faith development at a Disciples congregation in Medford, Oregon. She is preparing for a research project in psychology that will measure the impact of "the closet" on children. She is also a clergy member of the California/Nevada Conference of the United Methodist Church.

Mark Reeve is a member of Trinity United Methodist Church, Atlanta, Georgia, where he helps lead Disciple Bible Study. He is also active with Bi-Net Atlanta.

Daniel Rosemergy has been pastor of the Brookmeade Congregational Church, United Church of Christ, in Nashville, Tennessee, since 1982. He is a second-career minister with a background in higher education administration and a graduate of Vanderbilt University Divinity School.

H. David Stewart has served as pastor of Dayton Avenue Presbyterian Church in Saint Paul, Minnesota, since 1985. He is a graduate of San Francisco Theological Seminary and Occidental College.

Sylvia Thorson-Smith is a lecturer in religious studies and sociology at Grinnell College in Grinnell, Iowa. She has written and spoken extensively on sexuality issues for the Presbyterian Church (U.S.A.).

Christine Trenholm is a retired high school teacher and was chairperson of the Open and Affirming Study Group at First Congregational Church, Greenfield, Massachusetts.